Alex Callinicos

Southern Africa after Zimbabwe

First published 1981 by Pluto Press Limited,
Unit 10 Spencer Court, 7 Chalcot Road, London NW1 8LH

ISBN 0 86104 336 7

Cover designed by Terry Seago
Cover picture by permission of International Defence and Aid Fund
Map on page iv by Malcolm Swanston & Associates, Derby

Typeset by Grassroots Typeset, London NW6 (tel: 01-328 0318)
Printed in Great Britain by Photobooks (Bristol) Limited,
28 Midland Road, St Philips, Bristol.

Contents

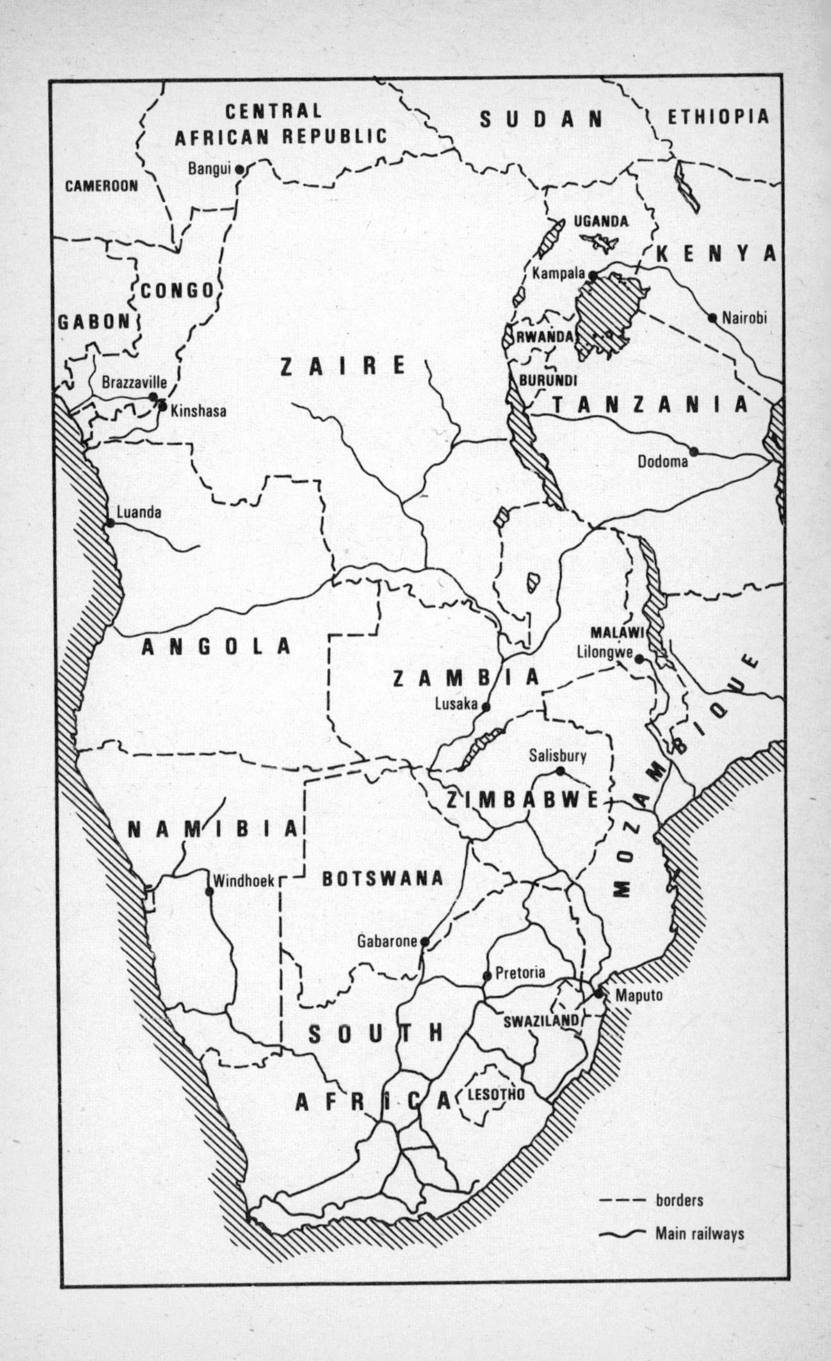
CENTRAL AFRICAN REPUBLIC
SUDAN
ETHIOPIA
Bangui
CAMEROON
UGANDA
KENYA
Kampala
CONGO
GABON
Nairobi
RWANDA
ZAIRE
BURUNDI
Brazzaville
Kinshasa
TANZANIA
Dodoma
Luanda
MALAWI
Lilongwe
ANGOLA
ZAMBIA
Lusaka
MOZAMBIQUE
Salisbury
ZIMBABWE
NAMIBIA
Windhoek
BOTSWANA
Gabarone
Pretoria
Maputo
SWAZILAND
SOUTH AFRICA
LESOTHO
borders
Main railways

Preface

This book is intended in part as a sequel to *Southern Africa after Soweto* which John Rogers and I wrote in the immediate aftermath of the June 1976 revolt. I hope that it can stand in its own right, although much more historical detail will be found in the earlier book.

I am grateful to Chris Harman and Mike Kidron, who between them suggested I write this book; to Richard Kuper for showing great patience and making many very helpful editorial suggestions; to John Rogers and others with whom I discussed the book and who made comments on drafts; to Tim Sheehy, David Caute and my other companions during the funeral rites of white Rhodesia; and to the Master and Fellows of St Peter's College, Oxford. Of course, only I am responsible for the result.

Alex Callinicos
November 1980

Abbreviations

ANC	African National Congress (South Africa) African National Council (Zimbabwe)
AZAPO	Azanian African People's Organisation
BAD	Department of Bantu Administration and Development (now Co-operation and Development)
BCM	Black consciousness movement
BMWU	Black Municipality Workers Union
BOSS	Bureau of State Security (now National Intelligence Service)
BPC	Black People's Convention
CYL	City Youth League
FCWU	Food and Canning Workers Union
FNLA	National Front for the Liberation of Angola
FOSATU	Federation of South African Trade Unions
Frelimo	Front for the Liberation of Mozambique
FROLIZI	Front for the Liberation of Zimbabwe
HNP	Herstigte Nasionale Partie (Purified National Party)
MPLA	Popular Movement for the Liberation of Angola
MWU	Mine Workers Union
NAFCOC	National African Federation of Chambers of Commerce
NUCW	National Union of Clothing Workers
NUMARWOSA	National Union of Motor Assembly and Rubber Workers of South Africa
NUSAS	National Union of South African Students
OAU	Organisation of African Unity
PAC	Pan Africanist Congress
PEBCO	Port Elizabeth Black Civic Organisation
PF	Patriotic Front
RF	Rhodesian Front
RLI	Rhodesia Light Infantry
SACP	South African Communist Party
SACTU	South African Congress of Trade Unions
SADF	South African Defence Force
SAP	South African Police
SASM	South African Student Movement
SASO	South African Student Organisation
TTL	Tribal Trust Land
TUCSA	Trade Union Council of South Africa
UANC	United African National Council
UAW	United Automobile, Rubber and Allied Workers Union
UDI	Unilateral Declaration of Independence
UMSA	Unity Movement of South Africa
UNITA	National Union for the Total Independence of Angola
WPGWU	Western Province General Workers Union
ZANLA	Zimbabwe African National Liberation Army
ZANU	Zimbabwe African National Union
ZANU-PF	Zimbabwe African National Union - Patriotic Front
ZAPU	Zimbabwe African People's Union (now Patriotic Front)
ZIPRA	Zimbabwe People's Revolutionary Army
ZUPO	Zimbabwe United People's Organisation

Introduction

Wednesday, 27 February 1980 — the first day of the Zimbabwean general elections. At the main polling station in Salisbury's Harare township, an enormous queue of black voters awaited their turn impatiently. Walking along this winding line of people, we were welcomed by a chorus of cock-crows and cries of 'Jongwe!'. 'Jongwe' is the Shona for cock; this bird was the symbol of the Zimbabwe African National Union-Patriotic Front (ZANU-PF). At the end of the queue a crowd of those who had already voted sang and danced. The refrain was that they were tired and wanted to rest after coming all the way from Mozambique. It was from Mozambique that ZANU-PF's military wing had for the previous seven years waged a war of liberation against the white settler regime. The climactic phase of that struggle was now taking place, it seemed, peacefully, in the polling booths, while angry white police reservists looked on impotently, clutching their G-3 automatic rifles.

At the main polling station in Highfield township a vast, rapidly growing crowd of young blacks were chanting 'Pamberi neZANU-PF! Pasi neMadzajutsaku!' — 'Forward with ZANU-PF! Death to the auxiliaries!' The auxiliaries were the private army of Bishop Abel Muzorewa, nominal prime minister since the phoney 'internal settlement' elections of April 1979. Thirty thousand unemployed young thugs had been put into uniform, given guns and rudimentary training, and sent into the countryside in what proved to be a fruitless attempt to roll back ZANU-PF's influence. Under a tree ZANU-PF activists had set up a table where they sat advising people how to vote. The young woman in charge, radiant with confidence, told us: 'We're going to win, and then we'll hold a *big* party and *everyone* will be invited.'

She was right. Confounding the expectations of most

observers, ZANU-PF won a landslide victory, capturing 57 out of the 80 African seats in the House of Assembly. Muzorewa was swept into oblivion and even Joshua Nkomo, historic leader of African nationalism in Zimbabwe, found himself reduced to second place. The hour was ZANU-PF's and their president, Robert Mugabe, became the prime minister of the independent state of Zimbabwe.

There was even a big party — although not everyone was invited. The official ceremony at which 90 years of British-sanctioned settler rule came to an end at midnight on 17 April 1980 took place at the Rufaro stadium in Harare. The stadium was packed with local and foreign dignataries — including Prince Charles, Indira Gandhi, Julius Nyerere, President Zia of Pakistan. Outside a mass of ordinary Zimbabweans pressed at the gates, demanding to be let in. The police used tear gas to drive them away. One participant in the ceremony later described the incident as 'a symbol of what the new government had most to fear ... any inability to satisfy the aspirations of their followers'.[1]

ZANU-PF's victory proved to be highly ambiguous. Mugabe told an interviewer that 'we would wish to be known as a government which is people-oriented; we work for the people and we serve the people. Socialism is our by-word.'[2] However, in practice his government immediately set out to conciliate western capital and the local white population and to restrain the strike wave which their election stimulated. Most significant of all, perhaps, was the willingness of ZANU-PF to leave largely unchanged the state apparatus inherited from the settlers. Symbolic of this policy was Mugabe's decision to place Lieutenant-General Peter Walls in charge of the Zimbabwe High Command. Walls had been commander of combined operations under both Ian Smith and Abel Muzorewa, and in this capacity had directed the ferocious white war effort against the guerillas. Only a few months previously ZANU-PF's official organ had declared:

> The Smith-Walls state machinery which the British government is eager to maintain must be dismantled. It is criminal to promote the myth that this murderous machinery can be converted by a conference at Lancaster House into serving the same people it presently massacres,

> tortures and maims day and night.[3]

This volte-face led to a marked change in Mugabe's international image. The most intelligent journal of business opinion in southern Africa, the Johannesburg *Financial Mail*, had before the election backed Muzorewa as 'the best hope for stability in our generation' in an editorial entitled 'Stem this marxist tide'. Its cover the issue after the election asked: 'Mugabe — Force for Stability?'.[4] And Lord Soames, British governor during the transition to majority rule, who before the elections made no secret of his dislike for both Mugabe's person and his politics, later revised his opinion. He said of Mugabe after his return to Britain:

> When he got in, he showed himself far more pragmatic and far more interested in keeping the economy of the country going — as opposed to bringing about rapid revolutionary change — than had seemed likely earlier on.[5]

And even Enos Nkala, Zimbabwean Minister of Finance and reputed to be one of the new government's radicals, referred to ZANU-PF's 'mild and pragmatic' socialism when introducing his first budget, which was described by *The Times* as including 'no radical changes or nasty surprises'.[6]

Yet all this should not be allowed to obscure the dramatic nature of events in Zimbabwe. Ian Smith had told a press conference on 20 March 1976: 'I don't believe in majority rule, black majority rule, ever in Rhodesia, not in a thousand years'.[7] Black majority rule had come within less than four years. The white colony's founder, Cecil Rhodes, no longer dominates Salisbury's main thoroughfare. His statue has been removed and Jameson Avenue, called after his closest collaborator, Rhodesia's first ruler, has been renamed Samora Machel Avenue in honour of the President of Mozambique, without whose backing ZANU-PF could never have succeeded. Ian Smith's old offices in Milton Buildings, next to where Rhodes's statue stood, are now occupied by a man regarded as a 'communist terrorist' by the settlers. And the party in power is not the collection of black crooks and fat-cats who gathered around Muzorewa but a movement steeled by years of repression and armed struggle which had adopted as its official ideology 'marxism-leninism-mao-tse-tung-thought'.

There were some western opinion-formers who saw the victory of ZANU-PF as an unmitigated disaster. Peregrine Worsthorne, a lucid if eccentric spokesman of the Tory right, regarded the Zimbabwean independence celebrations with a jaundiced eye: 'as well celebrate a backward leap into the heart of darkness'. He comforted himself with the reflection that 'fortunately — from the western point of view — there remains one solid instrument still capable of exerting some rational leverage on this latest box of black mischief — white South Africa'. 'The independence celebrated last week was more apparent than real', he continued,

> Britain's shadowy suzerainty making way for one from Pretoria which will have far more substance to it, rather as the end of Spanish rule in Latin America paved the way for Washington's incomparably more effective sway ... Enter a genuine colossus in the all too solid figure of the South African Prime Minister.[8]

Indeed, there seemed some prospect of this happening. Since taking office in September 1978, P.W. Botha had directed the South African regime on a new course. Placing 'national security' and survival above all else, he sought to shore up white power, shaken by the crisis of the 1970s, on firmer foundations. Wide ranging proposals for the reorganisation of the apartheid system, embodied in the reports of the Wiehahn and Riekert commissions, had been published in May 1979. Their aim was, through a variety of concessions, to incorporate the black middle classes and even sections of the black working class into the existing power structure. Externally, Botha combined a reliance on military strength with plans to create a 'constellation' of states, black and white, in southern Africa. The inertia and reliance on blind repression of Vorster's later years seemed to have been replaced by much greater vigour and flexibility.

The colossus, however, turned out to have feet of clay. Muzorewa's defeat was a serious blow for the South African regime — they had confidently expected that he would win. 'I can't understand how we were so misinformed. I just can't understand it', was the response of one senior South African official. 'The defeat of Bishop Muzorewa exposed a failure of intelligence as bad as the American failure in Iran', wrote Ken Owen in the Johannesburg *Sunday Times*. 'How could a government have been so wrong?'[9] Worse was to come.

The effect of Zimbabwe on Soweto was electric. This vast black township outside Johannesburg, the largest African city south of the equator, had been licking its wounds since the bloodbath which followed the uprising of 1976. Now that changed. 'After the riots of 1976 there was a mood of despair in Soweto. That's been completely removed by Mugabe's victory', Fanyana Mazibuko, secretary of the Soweto Teachers' Action Committee told Jonathan Steele of *The Guardian*.[10] The tide of black liberation seemed unstoppable. But it was not in Soweto, but a thousand miles to the south in the townships of the Cape, that the struggle begun in 1976 was resumed. As Zimbabwe's independence was celebrated, 100,000 coloured pupils in the Cape launched a boycott of their schools. Initially the regime's response was quite mild, at least by the brutal standards set by the South African police in 1976. Then, on Tuesday 17 June, the coloured townships around Cape Town exploded in a burst of rage. The commissioner of police, General Mike Geldenhuys, warned the rioters to 'expect no mercy' and authorised his men to shoot to kill.

This report of the police response by a British journalist noted for his pro-South African sympathies gives something of the flavour of life under P.W. Botha, suggesting that little has changed since Verwoerd and Vorster:

> Weary South African riot police in camouflage fatigues were drinking coffee in a police station in one of Cape Town's northern suburbs on Tuesday night when the telephone rang.
>
> A sergeant who looked like Ernest Borgnine picked up the phone, listened carefully and then nodded his shaggy head, grinning broadly.
>
> He put down the receiver and announced: 'The general says we can shoot to kill.'
>
> Everyone cheered, someone yelled 'Vrystaat!', an old Boer battle cry more often shouted on rugby fields these days ...
>
> The riot squad, looking like giants refreshed, stormed

> out and climbed into their vehicles.[11]

The *Cape Times* estimated that more than 40 people died and more than 200 were injured that night. According to one report, the police, armed with 'shotguns and automatic weapons', at one stage were going round the streets firing at random.

> One resident of Elsies River [township] told how police disgorged from a truck outside of his house and started shooting wildly into the darkened street in front of them. The screams that followed the shooting made it clear that some of their shots had found targets.[12]

Yet the regime found itself challenged on a much broader front than ever before. June 1980 began with the spectacular sabotage of installations belonging to the state-owned Sasol coal-into-oil project near Johannesburg. This incident dramatised the growth in armed actions against the white state by the guerillas of the banned African National Congress. And the black workers' movement, dormant since the mid-1970s, launched a wave of strikes which probably surpassed the record year of 1973. Every major centre — Johannesburg, Durban, Port Elizabeth-Uitenhage, and Cape Town — was affected, and a number of significant victories over the employers were won. The strike wave was an especially serious challenge to the regime since the aim of the Wiehahn report had been to confer official recognition upon, and at the same time embrace within the state-controlled industrial relations machinery, the independent black trade unions which had come into existence since 1973. When this policy did not lead speedily to industrial peace, strikers were given a taste of repression — most notably at the end of July 1980, when Johannesburg city council deported back to the bantustans striking migrant workers supporting the unofficial Black Municipality Workers Union.

This, then, was southern Africa at the start of the 1980s. Events had moved fast since the attempts in 1974-75 to arrive at detente between white South Africa and black Africa. This policy was symbolised by its two chief protagonists, John Vorster, the South African prime minister, and Kenneth Kaunda, president of Zambia, who had been prepared to abandon their respective clients — the white settlers and black nationalists of Zimbabwe — in the search for peace and economic co-operation. Detente is long since dead, a victim of the Angolan war. The confrontation between white power and black liberation continues, but its front line has now shifted to the Limpopo, separating Zimbabwe and South Africa.

The new situation can also be summed up in two men — Pieter Botha and Robert Mugabe, leaders of the two most powerful states in the region, the one architect of an immense and sophisticated military machine designed to crush African liberation movements, the other thrust to power by his leadership of just such a movement. The ambiguities of their respective positions summarise the contradictions in which southern Africa is caught. Botha is committed to a programme of reforms whose very goal, the preservation of the essentials of white power, rules out any hope of success, while Mugabe tries to incorporate within the existing structure of economic and political power a movement pledged to the destruction of that order. It is an explosive situation.

This book has two main aims: first, to trace the origins of ZANU-PF's victory and to assess its precise character and second, to analyse the context within which the confrontation between white capital and black labour in South Africa is unfolding. As John Rogers and I argued in our *Southern Africa after Soweto*; these developments must be understood in the light of 'western domination of the region' which:

> operates through the existence in South Africa of a powerful capitalist state whose political, economic and military influence spreads far beyond its borders, deep into black Africa ... The resolution of the crisis of southern Africa, a crisis that reaches as far as Lusaka and Kinshasa, lies in the hands of the massive black working class concentrated in the townships and mine-compounds of South Africa.[13]

1. A Region in Crisis

On 17 September 1976 Henry Kissinger, United States Secretary of State, flew into Pretoria, administrative capital of South Africa. The first volume of Kissinger's memoirs, which deals with the early 1970s, contains not one reference to southern Africa, suggesting that this region figured rather low on his list of priorities.[1] Only the unfolding crisis in the region after 1974, and in particular the intervention of Russia and Cuba in Angola, forced Kissinger to devote an increasingly large portion of his energies to restoring stability in southern Africa. His visit to South Africa (greeted with derision by Soweto students, who called him 'Kiss inja', 'kiss a dog') was the first stage in a sustained diplomatic offensive by the western powers designed to take the heat out of the confrontation between black and white, an offensive whose chief fruit to date has been the Lancaster House agreement of 21 December 1979, which ended the war in Zimbabwe and paved the way for Robert Mugabe's electoral triumph. In order to understand this offensive we need to consider, first, the nature of the political crisis which burst upon southern Africa in the mid-1970s and the failure of local attempts to resolve it, and, second, the western interests in the region which made intervention imperative.

The Failure of Detente

The overthrow on 25 April 1974 of the Portuguese dictatorship by a group of radical army officers pledged to end the colonial wars in Africa rendered untenable the prevailing order in southern Africa. The heart of this order, South Africa, had been protected from the threat of guerilla incursions by a chain of white-ruled buffer states, embracing Pretoria's own colony of South West Africa, the settler state in Rhodesia, and the two Portuguese 'overseas provinces' of Angola and Mozambique.

The most serious threat to that order came in the latter two territories, where black freedom fighters were engaged in a ferocious struggle with the colonial power in Lisbon. Although military victory for the guerillas was by no means certain in April 1974 — Frelimo (the Front for the Liberation of Mozambique) had not succeeded in penetrating the southern and more urbanised portion of the colony, while divisions between the liberation movements in Angola played into the enemy's hands — the pressure of the war drained the Portuguese economy and bred growing discontent in the barracks. The April coup had the support of important sections of Portuguese capital, increasingly geared to the Western European economy rather than the African colonies, as well as the mass of the working population.

For the surviving white regimes in southern Africa, however, the situation had changed suddenly and drastically for the worst. It was bad enough for South Africa, which relied on Mozambique for 100,000 mineworkers and access to the sea via the port of Lourenco Marques (soon renamed Maputo) for the industries of the Witwatersrand. For the Smith regime in Rhodesia, sharing a long common border with Mozambique, the prospect of a Frelimo government in Maputo, which came to pass in June 1975, was nothing less than catastrophic. Since December 1972 guerillas belonging to the Zimbabwe African National Liberation Army (ZANLA), ZANU's military wing, had been operating in the north-east of Rhodesia from bases provided for them by Frelimo. Now Ian Smith's entire southern flank had been turned. The probability of an eventual guerilla victory had increased greatly.

The new situation brought to the surface implicit tensions between Salisbury and Pretoria. The ruling Rhodesian Front had been swept to power in December 1962 by a coalition of white forces in which the farmers prevailed with the support of 'the "small man", the clerks, shop assistants, artisans to whom African advancement presented the greatest threat'.[2] These groups were united in their opposition to African nationalism and to the attempts by the British government, with the support of the multinational companies which dominated the colony's economy, to lay the basis for an eventual transfer of power to the black middle class.[3]

In April 1964 Ian Smith replaced the more conciliatory

Winston Field as prime minister. On 11 November 1965 he issued a unilateral declaration of independence from Britain, with, in the words of a British Conservative historian not unsympathetic to the settlers, 'the unavowed purpose' of introducing 'a form of apartheid'.[4]

The British government of the day, under Harold Wilson, had already ruled out the use of force to suppress a white rebellion and relied on the imposition of economic sanctions to bring Smith to heel. To succeed, this policy depended on the support of the South African regime. This was not forthcoming. The South African prime minister at the time of UDI, Hendrik Verwoerd, and his successor, John Vorster, were both unenthusiastic about the white rebellion on their northern border. However, strategic and domestic political considerations dictated that they sustain the Smith regime both economically and, after the first major guerilla offensive in 1967, militarily.

The Portuguese coup created a widening gap between the interests of Pretoria and her Rhodesian clients. Vorster and his closest advisers decided to seek a *modus vivendi* with the new Frelimo regime effectively in control of Mozambique from September 1974. This policy was widened out into an ambitious strategy of detente with black Africa, whose purpose was to achieve a political accommodation with the rulers of the frontline states — Zambia, Tanzania and Botswana, soon to be joined by Angola and Mozambique.

Although it was occasioned by the Portuguese coup and its reverberations, there were more long-term economic forces at work behind detente. South African manufacturing industry suffers from the restricted nature of internal demand caused by the low level of black wages, as well as from low productivity which makes South African manufactured exports uncompetitive in the world market. The most obvious local markets for these goods are those of southern and central Africa. But these were and largely remain closed to South Africa because of black opposition to apartheid. The continued expansion of South African capitalism is closely bound up with a political settlement with black Africa.[5]

Short-term economic factors also played their part. The Zambian economy was by 1975 near to collapse. The price of copper, to which Zambia owes 90 per cent of its foreign earnings, had fallen as a result of the world recession to levels which made it uneconomic for the copper mines to continue producing. The disastrous condition of agriculture made the country increasingly dependent on imported food, while the closure of the Rhodesian border in 1973 and of the Benguela railway in 1975 placed land-locked Zambia in an increasingly desperate situation. A Rhodesian settlement would re-open the border, while detente with Pretoria would give Zambia access to South African loans and exports. No wonder that Kenneth Kaunda — his hopes of building a self-sufficient Zambian economy in ruins — seized on detente with an eagerness born of desperation.[6]

The terms of detente were simple: Vorster would use his influence on the Salisbury regime to secure a peaceful transition to majority rule in Zimbabwe, while the frontline presidents, and in particular Kaunda and Julius Nyerere of Tanzania, would ensure the co-operation of the Zimbabwean nationalists. Vorster's aim, which Kaunda tacitly accepted, was to replace the Rhodesian Front with a black regime which would respect South African hegemony and western economic interests. The new alliance bore fruit in the Lusaka agreement of 7 December 1974, under the terms of which the Zimbabwean nationalist leaders, many of them recalled from Rhodesian prison for the occasion, undertook to unite within the framework of the African National Council headed by Bishop Abel Muzorewa in order to negotiate a settlement with a reluctant Ian Smith.[7]

Detente did not fail for want of trying on Vorster's and Kaunda's parts. The close collaboration between the two men was highlighted on 25 August 1975 when they met at the Victoria Falls in an abortive attempt to screw an agreement out of Smith and the nationalists. Kaunda used the pretext of the murder of Herbert Chitepo, the ZANU chairman, to gaol over a thousand Zambian-based ZANLA guerillas in March 1975 in the hope of breaking the opposition to detente. Vorster withdrew the South African troops stationed in Rhodesia in August 1975, a move aimed at Smith. And there is evidence that the decision to commit South African troops to Angola was taken in part at Kaunda's behest.[8]

Yet Angola was the rock upon which the Vorster-Kaunda alliance foundered. The roots of the 1975-76 war lay in the fact that in Angola, unlike Mozambique, no single liberation movement prevailed. Instead three groups competed for hegemony: the Popular Movement for the Liberation of Angola (MPLA) with strong support among the urban masses of Luanda as well as the backing of the Soviet Union; the National Front for the Liberation of Angola (FNLA), formed among the northern Bakongo and enjoying a long-standing relationship with the Mobuto regime in Zaire and its CIA backers; and the southern-based National Union for the Total Independence of Angola (UNITA) whose charismatic leader, Jonas Savimbi, contracted a marriage of convenience with Pretoria. The west and the South Africans, worried about retaining control of Angola's wealth in oil and other raw materials, sought to exclude MPLA from power and therefore gave their backing to FNLA and UNITA, ready instruments for their purpose. When covert intervention by the South African Bureau of State Security (BOSS) and western intelligence services, notably the CIA, failed to deliver the goods, South African troops were committed. The balance was, however, tipped in MPLA's favour by an influx of Soviet war materials and Cuban troops. The Ford administration in Washington, who had encouraged the South Africans to invade in the first place, were unable to prevent the American senate cutting off further funds for their intervention in Angola, and Pretoria withdrew its troops in February 1976.[9]

The effects of the Angolan war were incalculable. Relations between the US and South Africa were embittered; Vorster and Piet Botha, his Minister of Defence, felt stabbed in the back by Kissinger. South African blacks rejoiced to see their masters humiliated. Detente was killed stone dead, in public at least. The frontline presidents hardened their position. Angola strengthened the hand of President Julius Nyerere of Tanzania, who had been arguing for some time that a resumption of the armed struggle was necessary to force Smith into serious negotiations. Nyerere had been the leading supporter of MPLA during the 1975-76 war, and he now had the backing in the frontline leaders' counsels of two radicals, Samora Machel of Mozambique and Agostinho Neto of Angola. At a meeting in Quelimane, Mozambique, on 7-8 February 1976 the frontline presidents re-affirmed their support for the armed struggle. The following month Mozambique closed its border with Rhodesia, as a token of the Frelimo government's commitment to the new guerilla offensive. Yet Nyerere's objective remained a negotiated settlement — 'we are building up the pressure to deliver Smith to London', he told an interviewer[10] — even if for the moment armed struggle was to take priority.

From Kissinger to Carter

As Nyerere's reference to London suggests, the western powers were now drawn onto the centre of the stage in southern Africa, where previously they had been quite happy to let Vorster and Kaunda make the running (a policy of benign neglect of the region and tacit encouragement of links between Pretoria and black Africa had been outlined in a 1969 National Security Council memorandum prepared under Kissinger's supervision).[11] The new interest taken by Washington in southern Africa reflected two major considerations. First, there was concern about the security of the advanced capitalist countries' investments and sources of new materials in the region. What Cyrus Vance, who succeeded Kissinger as secretary of state in the Carter administration, said of the continent as a whole was true of southern Africa in particular:

> Africa's mineral and agricultural wealth already provides a substantial portion of our own imports of such commodities as copper, cobalt and manganese for our industries, and cocoa and coffee for our homes. And Africa supplies 38 per cent of our crude petroleum imports.[12]

Even South Africa, the most industrialised country in the continent, is of importance to the west first and foremost as a producer of crucial raw materials (see Table 1). There were also considerable western investments to worry about: in 1976 South Africa's foreign liabilities amounted to nearly R20 billion, 37 per cent to the UK, 21 per cent to the US, 9 per cent to West Germany, 5 per cent to Switzerland, and 4 per cent to France.[13]

Second, there was the fear that the crisis of the white regimes would give the USSR and its allies an opening in an area previously part of the western camp. To some extent these fears had already been realised in Angola. Kissinger had denounced Russian and Cuban intervention there as 'an ominous precedent ... of grave consequence even if the intervention occurs in a seemingly remote area. Such a precedent cannot be

Table 1: Mineral Reserves and Production

	World reserves		World production	
	percentages			
	SA	USSR	SA	USSR
Platinum Group	86	13	55	31
Chrome Ore	83	1	30	32
Vanadium	64	33	46	20
Manganese Ore	48	45	24	35
Gold	49	19	59	19
Fluorspar	46	4	5	11
Asbestos	10	25	10	36
Uranium	17	13	13	28

Source: *Financial Times*, 25 October 1978.

tolerated.'[14] Once Angola had been 'lost', western attention switched to Zimbabwe, where it was feared that the armed struggle, if continued, would lead to social revolution and, possibly, a confrontation between the super-powers. The late Anthony Crosland, then British foreign secretary, told the NATO Council in December 1976:

> If the issue were settled on the battlefield, it would seriously lessen the chances of bringing about a moderate regime in Rhodesia and would open the way for more radical solutions and external interventions on the part of others.[15]

Hence the American secretary of state's new interest in the 'seemingly remote area' of southern Africa. His most urgent task was to end the war in Zimbabwe. This involved taking up the broken threads of detente — after Angola, negotiations between black Africa and Pretoria could take place only under the aegis of an outside power. Kissinger toured black Africa in April 1976, denouncing apartheid to pacify his audiences. He met Vorster in Munich in June and in Zurich in September, while South Africa's townships burned. It seems that the outline of a deal was hammered out. Vorster would use his control of Rhodesia's supplies of oil and other essential imports to force Smith to the negotiating table, while Kissinger would square the Africans. Moreover, Kissinger would take the odium for forcing Smith to accept majority rule, protecting Vorster from any domestic white backlash provoked by a 'betrayal' of the Rhodesian settlers.[16]

In the short term this strategy worked. Vorster tightened the screws. Ted Sutton-Pryce, a deputy minister in Smith's office, told a Rhodesian Front closed meeting that 'Vorster is the bad guy' and reported that fuel supplies were down to 19.6 days when Kissinger arrived in Pretoria.[17] When the Rhodesian security forces attacked the ZANLA base at Nyadzonya in Mozambique, killing 1,200 people, Vorster immediately terminated Operation Polo under which South African military personnel was secretly supplied to the regime, thus cutting Smith's air-strike capacity by half.[18] When he met Kissinger and Vorster in Pretoria on 19 September Smith was a beaten man. Although he described the American proposals as 'my suicide note', he signed them, and on 24 September 1976 broadcast to Rhodesian whites, telling them that majority rule would be introduced within two years.

Characteristically, the agreement signed in Pretoria was riddled with ambiguities, particularly as far as the arrangements for the transition to majority rule were concerned. The proposals provided for a joint black-white government to preside over the transition — but who would have the final say? And who would control the army and police? These issues, which Kissinger fudged over, hoodwinking both sides in the process, led to the failure of the Geneva conference, convened under British chairmanship to settle the details of the Pretoria agreement. Perhaps Kissinger could have bridged the differences, but within a few days of the conference opening on 28 October 1976 Gerald Ford had lost the presidential elections to Jimmy Carter and Kissinger was a lame duck secretary. After seven weeks of bickering and manoeuvring the Geneva conference adjourned on 14 December, never to be reconvened. The Pretoria agreement proved even more short-lived than Kissinger's other 'miracles' in Indo-china and the Middle East.[19]

It was left to the incoming Carter administration and to the British government, drawn into the proceedings by its residual status as colonial power in Rhodesia and by its considerable economic interests in the region, to pick up the pieces. Here, however, southern Africa became drawn into a wider reappraisal of western strategy by the new administration. Although Carter's 'human rights' policy was soon to be displaced by a straightforward cold-war stance, it was to have an important impact in southern Africa. The policy had been formulated in the mid-1970s by the Trilateral Commission, a body sponsored by David Rockefeller, chairman of the Chase Manhattan Bank and one of the lynchpins of the East Coast establishment, on which Carter and much of his cabinet had served. The aim was to develop a new strategy that would enable American capitalism to adjust to the new balance of economic and political forces produced by Vietnam and the crisis of the mid-1970s.

Some of the thinking behind this policy was spelt out by Zbigniew Brzezinski, soon to be presidential national security adviser, in an article published shortly before Carter's election. He was concerned chiefly with the fact that ideologically the US was on the defensive. The American 'libertarian myth' which had animated the cold war struggle against Moscow had been undermined, especially by the rise of nationalism in the third world.

> Today, the traditional American values of individualism, free enterprise, the work ethic, and efficiency are contested both at home and even more abroad by statism, emphasis on the collective (national or societal), on social equity, and on welfare.

Kissinger's *realpolitik*, framed in terms of balance-of-power calculations, could not fill the ideological vacuum. Instead Washington should stress the virtues of 'pluralism' and 'diversity', and respond positively to 'global pressures for reform of existing international arrangements'.[20] It was a policy for a world in which American hegemony had been undermined, but where US capital possessed vast economic interests across the globe. In order to re-establish this shaken hegemony, the American establishment would have to come to terms with the now assertive capitalisms which had emerged in parts of the third world — the OPEC bloc, for example, and the 'newly industrialising countries' (Brazil, Taiwan, South Korea etc.) — and build closer links with their allies, and rivals, in western Europe and Japan.

In Africa, the new policy involved a 'tilt' away from South Africa and towards Nigeria. This political change reflected an important shift in the pattern of economic relationships on the continent. In 1976 US direct investment in South Africa amounted to $1,665 million, 37.3 per cent of the total for Africa. It was, however, growing much less rapidly there than in the rest of the continent. In 1976 new US investments in South Africa were only $9 million and re-invested earnings $73 million; the comparable figures for Africa as a whole were $256 million and $584 million.[21] In part, this was caused by western investors' doubts about South Africa's economic and political prospects. After Soweto and Angola foreign capital poured out of the country — there were net outflows of R1,293 million in 1978 and R3,082 million in 1979.[22] The changing balance of foreign investment in Africa also reflected the growing economic importance of Nigeria, whose oil revenues had made her a major market for western goods. US trade with Nigeria surpassed that with South Africa as long ago as 1973, while in 1978 Nigeria took UK exports worth £1,133 million (the comparable figure for South Africa was £667 million), making her Britain's ninth largest trading partner.[23] Moreover, Nigeria is the second largest supplier of crude oil to the US and accounts for 17 per cent of total US imports.[24]

A new element was thus added to western calculations about southern Africa. As Andrew Young, Carter's first ambassador to the United Nations put it, 'If we don't take an interest in human rights in southern Africa, we can't rely on Nigeria to supply oil'.[25] Brzezinski was more circumspect, but the basic message was the same:

> Nothing could be more destructive than for the United States to position itself as the ultimate shield of the remnants of white supremacy at a time when racial equality is coming to be accepted as an imperative norm. That would rally all of Africa and much of Afro-Asia against us.[26]

The new special relationship between Washington and Lagos was reflected in Carter's choice of Nigeria as the first African country to be visited by an American president in April 1978.

The extent of the shift in American policy was highlighted when Vorster met the US Vice-President, Walter Mondale, in Vienna in May 1977. Previous American criticisms of apartheid had been window dressing, concealing ineffectually the close links between Washington and Pretoria. But now Mondale, coordinator of US Africa policy, declared that:

> full participation by all citizens of South Africa — equal participation in the election of its national government and in its political affairs — is essential to a healthy, stable and secure South Africa.[27]

The South Africans reacted to this apparent call for black majority rule with fury. The foreign minister, Pik Botha, a *verlig* (enlightened) member of Vorster's cabinet, called it a 'commitment to suicide. No way. We shall not accept that; not now, not tomorrow, never, never.' Vorster called a general election on 30 November 1977 and won a sweeping mandate from the all-white electorate to oppose American 'strangulation by finesse'. Relations between Washington and Pretoria were further embittered by a row caused by Russian allegations that South Africa had detonated a nuclear device in the summer of 1977 and by US support for the mandatory embargo on the supply of arms to the apartheid regime imposed by the UN after the black consciousness movement had been banned on 19 October 1977.

The result was to strengthen the hand of those within the Nationalist establishment who wished to pursue a policy more independent of Washington. Their chief spokesman was the Minister of Defence, P.W. Botha, who succeeded Vorster in September 1978. Pretoria had already shifted towards 'internal settlements' with 'moderate' black leaders in Zimbabwe and Namibia, backing the governments such agreements produced against the guerillas. Vorster had resumed supplies to the Rhodesian regime after the Pretoria agreement, while Botha sent away (with a flea in their ears) the foreign ministers of the five western 'contact powers' who flew into Pretoria in October 1978 in an effort to strike a deal on the decolonisation of Namibia. He also broke with South Africa's tradition of military co-operation with NATO forces in the South Atlantic and Indian Ocean. According to *Newsweek*, 'shortly after his election, the prime minister served notice that South Africa wanted no part of NATO'. The navy — the service with the closest links with Britain and other western powers because of its role in protecting the Cape route — bore the brunt of this shift in policy, and was demoted to the status of junior partner in the South African Defence Force's (SADF) 'total strategy' aimed at repelling domestic insurgents and foreign invaders, losing its long-range frigates for Israeli strike craft designed for coastal defence and raids on neighbouring African ports.[28] South Africa's military strength was intended by Botha to underpin a 'constellation of states' in southern Africa that would clearly be intended to remain under Pretoria's thumb.

Without South Africa's leverage on the settlers in Zimbabwe and Namibia, the western powers lacked the power necessary to end the wars in these countries. The Anglo-American proposals on Zimbabwe, published in September 1977, provided for the integration of the guerillas and the Rhodesian security forces and for a British military and political presence during the transition to majority rule. They were stillborn, despite a visit to Salisbury by a mission headed by Cyrus Vance and the British Foreign Secretary, David Owen, in April 1978. Assured of Pretoria's backing, Smith could afford to ignore the west. Ironically, it was developments apparently favourable to the regime — the elections of April 1979 and the Tory victory in Britain — which were to lead to the Lancaster House agreement.

A New Scramble for Africa?

The American human rights offensive was in any case short-lived. One observer noted that:

> In late 1977 and early '78, a decided shift became apparent in the Carter administration's approach to southern Africa. The initial focus on peaceful transition to majority rule swung back to a revival of east vs. west confrontation politics in Africa. Instead of concentrating on putting an end to minority rule in the region, the Carter administration began to orchestrate a steady drumbeat of anti-Soviet and anti-Cuban statements.[29]

This shift reflected growing alarm in Washington concerning Soviet penetration of the US sphere of influence in Africa. Angola proved to be only the beginning.

One of America's most loyal allies in the continent, Emperor Haile Selassie of Ethiopia, was overthrown by the military in February 1973 against the background of a mass uprising against famine and inflation and the ruling Amharic oligarchy's unsuccessful attempt to hold onto the rebel province of Eritrea. Lieutenant-Colonel Mengistu Haile Mariam, who eventually came to dominate the ruling *derg* (junta), represented a group of officers drawn from the non-Amharic nationalities who make up a majority of the Ethiopian population. He was able to win popular support especially in the south of the country, where many of the vast estates of the Amharic nobility were broken up and handed over to the peasants. But the far left Ethiopian People's Revolutionary Party, which enjoyed considerable support among the workers and students of Addis Ababa, was ruthlessly suppressed. Moreover, the Eritrean independence movement was the victim of Mengistu's unremitting hostility, since the *derg* remained committed to preserving the unity of the state which they had inherited from the emperors.

The Ethiopian revolution, and the ensuing tensions throughout the Horn of Africa, led to a remarkable reversal of alliances on the part of the Soviet Union. Hitherto Somalia had been one of Moscow's closest allies in Africa. However, when in 1977 war broke out between Ethiopia and Somalia over the latter's claim to its neighbour's south-eastern province of Ogaden, Brezhnev switched sides. A major motive seems to have been Russian interest in Ethiopia's Red Sea ports, which would give the Soviet Navy access to a strip of water of vital strategic importance to Saudi Arabia, Egypt and Sudan, three of the most pro-western Arab states. This at least is what these remarks by a Soviet diplomat to a Somali official suggest:

> Mengistu Haile Mariam is a good boy. If socialism wins in Ethiopia we will have 30 million friends there plus the ports of Assab and Massawa. You Somalis are only three million.[30]

The only hitch lay in the fact that Assab and Massawa are in Eritrea, then virtually overrun by the rebels. US reluctance to support Mengistu's unsuccessful 1976 offensive against the Eritreans, who were receiving support from Saudi Arabia, probably motivated his decision to ally himself to Russia, announced on a visit to Moscow in May 1977. Soviet military assistance worth $2 billion, 14,000 Cuban troops, 11 Russian generals and a team of experts from the KGB and the East German Ministry of State Security were flown into Ethiopia. In November 1977 Siad Barre, president of Somalia, after prolonged wooing by Saudi Arabia and other conservative Arab regimes, broke off links with Moscow and appealed to the west for help. This did not prevent his crushing military defeat. The Soviet and Cuban forces were transferred to Eritrea where they succeeded in driving the rebels out of the cities they had captured, although it soon became clear that the war would be a long and tough business.

Closer to southern Africa there were further causes for alarm. Two attempts, in March 1977 and May 1978, by the forces of the National Front for the Liberation of the Congo (FNLC), a Zairean opposition movement based in Angola, to seize Zaire's Shaba province (formerly Katanga) sent a shiver of fear through western capitals. The corrupt and incompetent rule of General Mobutu Sese Soko, placed in power by the CIA, had led to a collapsing economy, rampant inflation and a bankrupt government.[31] Despite the undoubted popularity of the rebels, western investors (principally Belgium but other western European countries and the US were also involved) feared for their control of the country's raw materials — Zaire accounts fo 67 per cent of world production of cobalt, a mineral vital to the aircraft industry, and 8 per cent of world copper production.[32] The fall of Kolwezi, the country's main mining and manufacturing centre, in May 1978 created near-hysteria in Washington. The US 82nd Airborne Division was placed on special alert and an emergency NATO meeting called to discuss military intervention in Zaire. Carter accused Cuba of master-minding the invasion (although Fidel Castro later claimed that he had warned Washington of the danger of another war in Shaba beforehand). On 18 May, after consultation with Carter, President Giscard d'Estaing despatched 600 foreign legionnaires to Shaba. Closely followed by 1,000 Belgian paratroopers, they were able to recapture Kolwezi with little difficulty. The affair highlighted France's willingness to back up her economic interests in Africa with open military intervention, maintaining 12,500 troops and a chain of bases in her former colonies.[33]

To the crises in Zaire and on the Horn could be added a number of other disturbing factors: the Cuban presence in Angola; close relations between Mozambique and the eastern bloc (in March 1978 President Podgorny became the first major Soviet leader to set foot in southern Africa, when he visited

Mozambique); the aid given the Zimbabwe African People's Union (ZAPU) by Russia and her allies. Africa had become a cockpit in the new cold war between the super-powers. David Owen even accused Moscow of engaging in a new 'scramble for Africa'.

The reality was, of course, rather different. It was the crises of the western-imposed order in the continent which had given Russia an opening. The source of instability lay in the slow disintegration of the white regimes in the south, the corruption and brutality of most 'independent' black states, as well as in more general factors — the continent's continued dependent status as a supplier of raw materials to the advanced capitalist countries and the impact of world recession on African economies. Moscow was quick to exploit the crises that arose, and their cynical behaviour in the Horn showed the dangers of any strategy for change which relied on the 'socialist' countries for allies. The idea, however, that 'Soviet social imperialism' is the main threat to African independence is hardly plausible, given the reality of western domination of the continent and the extent to which the USSR's own vast natural resources largely duplicate those to be found in Africa (see Table 1).

The intensified competition between the super-powers, which led at the end of the 1970s to an effective resumption of the cold war with the NATO decision to deploy a new generation of 'theatre nuclear weapons' in Europe and the Soviet occupation of Afghanistan, could not leave Africa unaffected. The Iranian revolution and its aftermath were used to restore legitimacy to the idea of US military intervention abroad. Washington's decision to set up a Rapid Development Force, 200,000 at full strength, was taken with the Gulf in mind. The security of its oil-fields and of the regimes which presided over them was declared to be a 'vital interest' of the United States by Carter in January 1980. However, this force once established could be used in South Africa or Zaire should 'vital' western interests be threatened there. Egypt, Somalia and Kenya agreed to provide the RDF with bases. The new cold war could only be of benefit to the South African regime, which had long proclaimed its importance as a bulwark against communism in Africa. There were signs that Pretoria was extending feelers towards the west. Information on Russian submarine movements around the Cape was passed on from the SADF surveillance centre at Silvermine to NATO despite the row between Pretoria and Washington, and the South African military seemed eager to offer the US, busy expanding its Indian Ocean forces, facilities at Simonstown and Durban naval bases. 'You can talk about Kenya and Somalia, but no African country has our infrastructure', one senior naval officer told *Newsweek*.[34] Such military links would bring in their wake a greater western commitment to the apartheid regime's survival.

2. The Rise of Robert Mugabe

The main threat to western interests in southern Africa seemed to come in Zimbabwe, where the two wings of the Patriotic Front and in particular the Zimbabwe African National Union (ZANU), waged a bloody and heroic war of liberation against settler rule through much of the 1970s. To understand the nature of Robert Mugabe's electoral victory in March 1980 we must first consider the circumstances within which it arose.

White State, Black Resistance

The Zimbabwean people were the victims of conquest in a direct and brutal manner rare even in the history of imperialism in Africa. The occupation of the country by the British South Africa Company in 1890, the conquest of the Ndebele kingdom in 1893, the heroic uprising against the settlers of both Shona and Ndebele peoples in 1896 — the *chimurenga* — were fresh memories. The leaders of the nationalist movement were brought up among elders for whom both a free Zimbabwe and its brutal seizure were matters of direct experience.[1]

The society created by the conquest was based on the exclusion of the African majority from the best of the land. The Land Apportionment Act (1930) and its successor, the Land Tenure Act (1970), reserved roughly half the land for the whites, even though the ratio of black to white in Zimbabwe prior to independence was about 25:1. In a country where at the end of 1977 only 17 per cent of the population of nearly seven million lived in the main urban areas,[2] and where before the conquest access to land had been virtually unrestricted, this spelt disaster for the rural African economy (see Table 2 for land distribution). Most African peasants live in the Tribal Trust Lands (TTLs) reserved for them. There are some 675,000 cultivators in the TTLs, two and a half times the number which could work the land economically. By comparison, some 5,400 white farmers own roughly the same amount of land, heavily concentrated in the areas most suitable for productive farming. Traditional extensive agricultural methods, based on free access to land, have led in the TTLs to overstocking and soil erosion. Many African peasants find it impossible to support themselves and their dependents. In 1962-77 the maize grown in the TTLs fell from 352lb a head to 231lb, 40 per cent less than the amount necessary to meet subsistence needs. The real average income of rural households fell by 40 per cent between 1948 and 1970. It is estimated that half a million rural Africans living in the TTLs own no land at all.[3]

Table 2: Distribution of Rural Land and Population in Zimbabwe, 1976.

Land category	Acreage millions	% Land	African population (thousands)	European population
African farming land	43.66	53	4,440.6	2.3
European farming land	38.564	47	1,089.2	31.9

Source: R. Riddell, *The Land Question in Rhodesia* Gwelo: Mambo Press, 1978, pp. 34-35.

This situation had made possible a low-wage economy in Zimbabwe (see Table 3). Rural poverty means that 'between 50 and 60 per cent of all African households are dependent on income from employment as a main source of family income'.[4] At the same time the continued existence of a tribal rural economy provides a rudimentary social security system for the old, the sick and the unemployed, so that employers can pay wages less than those necessary to reproduce labour-power, and inhibits the formation of a settled African urban working class.

As a result, 'the low levels of wages force the vast majority of industrial workers to live in a constant state of poverty', while 'producers are able to benefit from low unit labour costs'.[5] The condition of black workers on the white farms, many of them contract labourers from neighbouring countries, is even more desperate.[6] At the same time the settlers, including the small white working class, enjoy one of the highest standards of living in the world, and plentiful black domestic servants.

Table 3: Employment and Earnings in Zimbabwe, 1977

	Employment thousands		Average annual earnings Zimbabwean dollars	
	African	European	African	European
Agriculture and forestry	342.3	5.7	232	5,737
Mining and quarrying	57.4	4.1	659	8,488
Manufacturing	126.9	20.8	918	6,678
Electricity and water	4.7	1.9	894	7,579
Construction	41.4	4.8	739	6,438
Transport & Communications	31.3	14.3	1,195	6,343
Public Administration	43.3	17.3	1,099	7,665
Education	29.5	7.1	1,271	5,437
Domestic service	123.0	—	424	—
Total*	901.0	117.0	588	6,156

* including categories not listed above

Source: *Economic Survey of Rhodesia, 1977*, Tables 12 and 13.

It was in this context of impoverishment and proletarianisation that the modern Zimbabwean nationalist movement emerged. The struggles of the nascent black proletariat — the Bulawayo railway strike of 1945 and the 1948 general strike — combined with discontent provoked by overcrowding in the black townships of Salisbury and Bulawayo, swelled to bursting point by the wartime expansion of manufacturing industry, and attempts by the state to impose individual tenure on African farmers set the scene for the City Youth League (CYL), formed in Harare in 1955 along lines modelled on the Youth League of the African National Congress (ANC) in South Africa. The dynamic and militant leadership of the CYL breathed life into the moribund local ANC, which was revived on 12 September 1957, the 67th anniversary of the white occupation of Salisbury. It was not James Chikerema or any of the other leaders of the Salisbury-based CYL who was chosen as ANC president, but, representing the group of Bulawayo trade unionists who made up the other main element in the new movement, Joshua Nkomo, ex-secretary of the African

Railway Workers' Union.

The ANC, forced to change its name several times as a result of government bannings, but finally known as the Zimbabwe African People's Union, found itself pushed into confrontation with the white regime which, even before the electoral victory of the Rhodesian Front (RF) in 1962, responded to African pressures with ever greater repression. Armed police were used to disperse a demonstration of 40,000 blacks who gathered in Salisbury in July 1960 to protest against the arrest of several nationalist leaders.

Differences over strategy led to a split within ZAPU. Nkomo was in favour of using diplomatic pressures in the UN and foreign capitals to screw from Whitehall the independence granted most of Britain's other African colonies. A rival group within the nationalist leadership — notably Ndabaningi Sithole, Robert Mugabe and Leopold Takawira — favoured militant action within Zimbabwe. The disagreements came to a head in August 1962, when Nkomo's opponents broke away from ZAPU to form the Zimbabwe African National Union (ZANU). The ensuing factional conflict undoubtedly helped the new RF regime impose its control, and after Ian Smith became prime minister in April 1964 the bulk of the leadership of both nationalist parties were rounded up and the organisations themselves banned. Ruthless repression enabled the regime to weather UDI without significant black opposition.[7] From exile the two liberation movements made attempts to overturn Smith by armed force. ZANU staged the first major armed action, the 'Sinoia Battles' of 27-28 April 1966, while ZAPU, in alliance with the South African ANC, mounted a sustained offensive based on the infiltration of guerilla bands across the Zambesi from Zambia between 1967 and 1970. Neither movement, despite the courage of their fighters, was able to shake the foundations of white power in this period. The armed struggle was still conceived of as a means of provoking British intervention rather than as a method of social revolution, and from 1967 onwards the settler forces were backed up by large contingents of South African Police. The failure of the armed offensives and the frustrations of exile led to dissensions among the nationalists abroad, giving rise to incidents such as the 11 March movement, an attempt by ZAPU fighters in 1971 to arrest their squabbling leaders (129 of the culprits were deported by the Zambian government to Rhodesia, where at least six were executed), and culminating in the formation later that year of a third group, the Front for Liberation of Zimbabwe (FROLIZI), by the losers in the ZAPU faction fight, James Chikerema and other leaders of the old CYL.[8]

Although the experience of repression, exile and armed struggle radicalised both ZANU and ZAPU, their basic character remained the same. They were both nationalist movements, committed to the establishment of an independent Zimbabwean state ruled on the basis of universal adult suffrage. The links ZAPU established with the Soviet bloc and with other liberation movements, such as the South African ANC, aligned to it, and by ZANU with China, did not alter this objective; for the left of both movements it was merely integrated into a stalinist stages theory in which the 'national-democratic' revolution against settler rule was strictly separate from, and must precede, the introduction of socialism.

The 1962 split was over methods, rather than objectives, and reflected the greater militancy of the ZANU leaders, their commitment to 'Confrontation, not Circumvention', as they put it. The subordination of class struggle to the 'national-democratic' revolution characteristic of both movements arose from the fact that their leadership was recruited from, and embodied the aspirations of, the black petty bourgeoisie. African teachers and businessmen in particular occupied an intermediate position, integrated into the white economy and state, yet denied advancement beyond a certain point and still part of the community from which they had sprung.[9] The black labour movement provided ZAPU in particular with many of its leaders, yet the fluidity of social relations, the close links between town and country, the relative lack of barriers between workers, small businessmen and intellectuals, meant that the black working class was submerged within a broader movement. In ZANU in particular intellectuals such as Ndabaningi Sithole, Robert Mugabe and Herbert Chitepo were the dominant figures. Internal disagreements were sometimes related to ethnic rather than political differences.

The Shona confederation of peoples make up 77 per cent of the population and have lived in Zimbabwe since around 1200. However, in the south-west of the country live the Ndebele, a Zulu offshoot which established a military state there in the early nineteenth century. With the Kalanga, Shona who became integrated into this state, the Ndebele make up 19 per cent of the population. Given that pre-capitalist relations of production in Zimbabwe were mediated through kinship relations, it is hardly surprising that these ethnic divisions should sometimes find political expression. ZANU has always been a predominantly Shona movement, while ZAPU, although drawn from both groups, has had an Ndebele-Kalanga hard core in its leadership.

ZANU and Detente

The 1970s began with the black resistance divided and in disarray. Their fortunes were transformed by two developments in 1972. First, an agreement between Smith and the British foreign secretary, Sir Alec Douglas-Home, which would have extended white supremacy well into the twenty-first century, provoked the first mass demonstrations in the black townships for a decade. So effective was the opposition orchestrated by the African National Council — an umbrella organisation headed by two hitherto unknown clerics, Bishop Abel Muzorewa and the Rev. Canaan Banana, but dominated by ZANU and ZAPU veterans — that Whitehall was forced to abandon the proposed settlement.[10] Hardly had white Rhodesia recovered from this blow when guerillas belonging to the Zimbabwe African National Liberation Army (ZANLA), ZANU's military wing, attacked a white farm in the north-eastern Centenary district on 21 December 1972. The offensive was conducted in alliance with Frelimo, which controlled the neighbouring Tete province of Mozambique. It marked the beginning of the war of liberation — the second *chimurenga* as ZANU called it after the 1896-7 uprising.[11] The fall of the Portuguese dictatorship, which meant that the guerillas would now have the support of a friendly government in Mozambique, made a peaceful settlement of the Zimbabwean conflict essential.

The chief obstacle to such an agreement proved to be the ZANU leadership, and especially those of the party executive who had spent the ten years before 1974 in Smith's prisons.[12] In 1970 six ZANU leaders held in Que Que Prison voted to depose Ndabaningi Sithole and replace him as party president with Robert Mugabe. When in November 1974 Sithole was summoned to meet the frontline presidents in Lusaka to discuss the implementation of the detente proposals agreed by Vorster and Kaunda, Mugabe and Moton Malianga appeared in his stead, much to the annoyance of the presidents who refused to recognise anyone but Sithole as leader of ZANU. The gaoled nationalists' attitude was summed up by Mugabe in a document written shortly after the Lusaka agreement was signed:

> We, ZANU leaders ... were very angry with Kaunda. We wondered how a man dedicated to Pan-Africanism and to our national cause could now [deal] with our enemy, Vorster. We think that Vorster understands only the language of the bullet![13]

The defiant attitude shown by Maurice Nyagumbo, who accompanied Sithole to another meeting in Lusaka, seems to have horrified even the ZANU military leaders. On Nyagumbo's account, Herbert Chitepo was in tears, while Josiah Tongogara, the ZANLA commander, sarcastically requested that 'the executive [in prison] should now tell them where to go with all the wounded who were in Zambia and where to train all our people now in the Tanzanian training camps.' Considerations of this sort forced the gaoled ZANU leaders grudgingly to accept the Lusaka agreement, especially when these were backed up by the threats of the frontline presidents. Samora Machel, Nyagumbo tells us:

> minced no words as to what he was going to do if we had maintained our decision; he was going to order the arrest of our two thousand five hundred fighting men ... in Mozambique. I must admit that President Machel was the only man who succeeded in intimidating me.[14]

These threats became reality when, in March 1975, after Chitepo had been killed by a car bomb, Kaunda arrested over 1,000 ZANLA fighters, including Tongogara and the bulk of the military leadership. The background to the Chitepo affair must be traced to the 1973 elections to the ZANU *Dare* (executive-in-exile), when older and more conservative leaders such as Noel Mukono and Simpson Mutambanengwe were replaced by a group of young radicals — Josiah Tongogara, Kumbirai Kangai, Rugare Gumbo, Mukudzei Mudzi and Mukutu Hamadziripi. The change reflected the huge growth in

ZANLA numbers caused by the war — the guerillas wanted a leadership more responsive to them and their aspirations. Tribal differences may also have played a role. Many of the members of the new *Dare* were Karanga, while Mukono and Mutambanengwe were Manyika, (both of which are Shona sub-groups). Those deposed retaliated by backing an attempt led by Thomas Nhari in December 1974 to overturn the *Dare*. It has been claimed that the Zambian government was implicated in the coup, which failed; certainly the assassination of Chitepo (who had played a somewhat ambiguous role in the Nhari affair, or so it was alleged) gave Kaunda an opportunity to eliminate one obstacle to detente — the *Dare* had been resisting attempts to integrate ZANLA into the ANC. During the Lancaster House conference a 'senior Rhodesian intelligence officer' confirmed that 'Tongogara had not been involved' in Chitepo's death and that the Nhari rebellion 'had followed secret meetings between dissident commanders and members of the Rhodesian Security Forces'.[15]

The temporary removal of the ZANU military leadership left a vacuum which various forces sought to fill. One such force was Muzorewa and Sithole who, after the collapse of negotiations with Smith, went abroad to drum up support for armed struggle under their leadership. In September 1975 Sithole formed the Zimbabwe Liberation Council in which he included the old FROLIZI leaders, Chikerema and Nyandoro. This bid for leadership ran afoul of the frontline presidents. As we saw in the previous chapter, the latter, under the guidance of Julius Nyerere, decided in the course of 1975 that a further dose of war was necessary to bring Smith round. But, Nyerere (with the support of Machel) argued, effective prosecution of the war meant getting rid of all old political leaders with their ambitions and squabbles, and building up a united organisation based on the guerillas. So ZIPA — the Zimbabwe People's Army — was launched. The ZANU guerillas held in Zambia were released in December 1975 and transferred to camps in Tanzania and Mozambique, where they were joined by ZAPU fighters. A joint military command divided equally between the two parties was established under Rex Nhongo, ZANLA commander in Tongogara's absence, and Nikita Mangena, his ZAPU opposite number. Effective control, however, was in the hands of Colonel Mbita, a Tanzanian officer who was also secretary of the OAU liberation committee — or so Sithole and Muzorewa claimed in a document where they complained of their forcible exclusion from the guerilla camps.[16]

That ZIPA in the end came to nothing owes much to the efforts of Robert Gabriel Mugabe. A few words must be said about this remarkable man. Born and educated at the Roman Catholic mission at Kutama,[17] Mugabe was a student at Fort Hare College in the Cape, breeding ground of South Africa's black elite, in 1949-51, when it was under the influence of the ANC Youth League. Anton Lembede, one of the League's founders, formulated the 'Africanist' ideology which continues to be a powerful force through its enduring influence on the black-consciousness movement. The League also produced the main leaders of the black resistance during the great battles of the 1950s and early 1960s — Nelson Mandela, Robert Sobukwe, Walter Sisulu, Oliver Tambo. Mugabe joined the Youth League and had his first encounter with marxism (of a sort) through his contact with white members of the South African Communist Party. Later, in 1958-60, he taught in Ghana, which had just achieved independence under the leadership of Kwame Nkrumah. He thus participated in two of the seminal experiences of post-war African nationalism. On his return to Rhodesia in 1960 Mugabe threw himself into the national movement and became the NDP's publicity secretary. He played an important role in the formation of ZANU, and became its secretary-general. Arrested in 1964, he used his time in gaol to study, adding no less than three degrees to his already impressive collection, and lost his only child. The experience must have consolidated his commitment to the radical nationalism which he came to embody after his release at the end of 1974.

In March 1975 Mugabe, accompanied by Edgar Tekere, slipped out of Zimbabwe to join the guerillas in Mozambique. They spent the months between April and September 1975 lost to the outside world in remote camps in the Mozambique bush, where they succeeded in assembling an army of 4,000 young guerillas. The Mozambicans then placed them in protective custody at Quelimane to keep them out of the way while ZIPA was formed.[18] However, the efforts to form a joint army proved to be a failure. The ZAPU elements withdrew after several bloody clashes with ZANU guerillas at Mgagao and Morogoro camps in Tanzania. ZIPA became effectively ZANLA in another guise. Sithole and Muzorewa alienated their potential supporters by including in the Zimbabwe Liberation Council the instigators of the Nhari rebellion of December 1974, Mukono and Mutambanengwe. A document by guerillas at Mgagao denounced Muzorewa and Sithole and declared their support for Mugabe.[19]

This situation helped to convince Nyerere and Machel that they should swing their support behind Mugabe as the most effective agent of the policy of using armed struggle to force Smith to the negotiating table. They may also have been influenced by the activities within the camps of a group of maoist radicals, notably Dzinashe Machingura and Elias Hondo, who were opposed to any negotiated settlement and who wished to transform ZIPA into 'a unique and revolutionary army ... [with the] strategic role of transforming itself into a political movement'[20] independent of all the old nationalist politicians — and of the frontline leaders. Tongogara and the other members of the ZANU *Dare* held in Zambia were released shortly before the opening of the Geneva Conference in October 1976. After the Conference broke up they returned to Mozambique and wrested control of the camps from Machingura and his allies, subordinating the guerillas to the ZANU leadership.[21]

In January 1977 Machingura, Hondo and 85 of their supporters were arrested by Mozambican troops. Mugabe felt sufficiently confident of his position to hold a party congress at Chimoio in September 1977, where he was formally elected ZANU president. Subsequently a section of the *Dare* itself — the so-called 'Gutu line', a predominantly Karanga group headed by Rugare Gumbo, Mukudzei Mudzi and Mukutu Hamadziripi — was arrested in January 1978, allegedly for advocating the fusion of ZANU and ZAPU and the establishment of closer links with Moscow. Thereafter Mugabe, flanked by Simon Muzenda and Edgar Tekere, respectively vice-president and secretary-general of ZANU, seemed firmly in control of both party and army. His standing had already been enhanced by the announcement on 9 October 1976 of the Patriotic Front, an alliance of ZANU and ZAPU. Nkomo had attempted after his release from detention to come to some agreement with Smith, but their negotiations finally collapsed in March 1976, when Mozambique closed its border with Rhodesia in line with the new strategy of military confrontation with the regime. Association with ZANLA, who had hitherto done much of the fighting, would undoubtedly enhance ZAPU's somewhat tattered credibility. Mugabe, on the other hand, needed the international recognition that would follow an alliance with Nkomo, far and away the best known Zimbabwean leader. The pact was, against all the odds, to survive even the February 1980 elections.

People's War Comes to Zimbabwe

The failure of detente was followed by a period in which endless diplomatic manoeuvres were pursued while the Zimbabwean countryside, where the mass of the population still live, was torn apart by the savage war fought between guerillas and security forces. ZANLA concentrated on the politicisation of the local peasants and farm-workers and on undermining the two main props of settler rule in the rural areas — the district commissioners and white farming communities. When the first ZANLA offensive began in December 1972, the settlers discovered that the guerillas had burrowed deep into the rotting structure of north-eastern Zimbabwe, an area notable for government neglect and the spectacularly unpopular eviction of the Tangwena tribe from their ancestral lands.

The regime reacted ruthlessly, imposing collective punishments on villages thought to be supporting the guerillas, moving peasants into 'protected villages' (PVs) — enclosed areas guarded by government troops like the strategic hamlets in Vietnam — and creating 'no-go areas' like the American free-fire zones in Vietnam. In July 1974 the entire population of Chiweshe Tribal Trust Land — 44,000 people — were moved into 21 PVs and subjected to a 6 a.m. to 6 p.m. curfew as part of Operation Overload, which was designed to separate the guerillas from the sea in which they swam. At their height, the PVs had half-a-million Africans confined within their fences.[22]

This strategy did not succeed. By May 1975 one well-informed observer could write that ZANU excercised 'a crude suzerainty over fair portions of Rhodesian soil'.[23] Detente, and the repression aimed at ZANU which it involved, led to a marked let-up in the struggle. However, thanks both to the efforts of Mugabe and Tekere and to the new policy of the frontline presidents, the guerillas took to the offensive in January 1976, this time not only in the north-east, but also in the east and the south-east. For the first time ZANLA was able to exploit the fact that Frelimo now controlled the whole of Mozambique. A further guerilla wave followed in April 1976, while fighters belonging to the Zimbabwe People's Revolutionary Army (ZIPRA), ZAPU's military wing, began to infiltrate from Botswana and Zambia. A series of raids were mounted on ZANLA bases in Mozambique. Selous Scouts (the regime's crack commando unit) in Frelimo uniforms raided Nyadzonya, just inside Mozambique, on 9 August, killing 1,200 people. During the Geneva conference guerillas, many of them teenagers with the most basic training, were poured in, leading to as many guerilla deaths during the seven weeks of the conference as in the whole of 1975. A series of raids by the security forces at the end of October 1976 destroyed six camps and 50 tons of weapons and ammunition in Tete province alone, but the guerillas had been forewarned and suffered only minor casualties.

The war continued to escalate for the next three years. The most important single development was the creation by ZANLA of a number of liberated zones in rural areas of Zimbabwe. Speaking at a conference in Brazzaville in August 1979 Mugabe claimed that 'the total population of the liberated zones is anything between 1.5 million and 2 million, out of a total population of 7 million.'[24] These zones were concentrated in Victoria, Manicaland and Mashonaland Central — the three provinces where ZANU-PF did best in the February 1980 elections. Mugabe described the functioning of areas under ZANLA control as follows:

> We organise our liberated areas and administer them on the principle of giving power to the people. In this regard, we create people's committees at the village and district levels, and charge such committees with the task of running collective projects in production and construction, education, health and sanitary work ... The popular essence of our struggle as a people's struggle is upheld by the creation of units of the militia force ... [which] complements and reinforces the National Liberation Army.[25]

The development of the liberated areas led Nathan

Shamuyarira, now Zimbabwean minister of information, to claim just before the 1980 elections began that 'in many rural areas the state machine was smashed' during the war.[26] If measured in damage caused to the structure of rural administration, then white power had been severely weakened. ZANLA was especially active in organising boycotts of schools and of cattle dipping. Eighty per cent of the 1,850 cattle dips in the TTLs were destroyed, causing a sharp rise in tick-borne cattle diseases;[27] by October 1979, 474,770 black pupils, 53 per cent of the total, had been displaced from their schools.[28] Guerilla activities had a devastating effect on white farming on the eastern border with Mozambique — by April 1979 some 2,000 white farms had been abandoned.[29]

Yet according to an excellent paper by Lionel Cliffe and Barry Munslow, ZANLA's achievement was to create 'not ... totally liberated regions but a patchwork of semi-liberated pockets in a majority of the TTLs'. This situation arose from the structure of class relations in Zimbabwe's countryside:

> In the neighbouring ex-Portuguese colonies, the war developed in the main in areas without a significant settler presence and whole regions became fully 'liberated areas'. This was not the case in Zimbabwe. The Land Apportionment Act and subsequent legislation had led to a massive occupation of land by settler farmers and at the same time created many discrete pockets of African reserves in the TTLs. Whole regions capable of generating and maintaining their own infrastructure and of isolating areas from any contact with a colonial regime, which to all intents and purposes was some hundreds of miles away, were a feature of say Mozambique's history of struggle ... Ingenuity and a somewhat different approach was required on the part of ZANU, faced as it was with this fragmented pattern of African reserves interspaced [sic] with white areas through which passed the major arteries of communication.[30]

This situation dictated ZANU's strategy — politicising the peasantry and attacking the local representatives of the regime, and especially the white farmers:

> Behind the ostensibly quiescent normal peasant daily

> existence of the TTLs, there grew up activities and structures of a system of dual power challenging the settler state. This was metaphorically — and frequently also literally — a difference of night and day. When darkness fell and the curfew laws camc into operation, entitling [sic] anyone leaving their homes to be shot by the security forces, villagers would sneak off to the agreed rendezvous for a meeting with local guerilla units. These meetings were virtually a nightly occurrence in many places. In these meetings politicisation occurred and problems not treated by the committee structures were heard and dealt with.[31]

Mediating between the guerillas and the peasants were the *mujibas* — young men acting as messengers and helpers for the ZANLA forces. Cliffe and Munslow describe the *mujiba* system as ZANU's 'unique contribution to the practice of people's war':

> The *mujibas* ... were the watchdogs of the ZANU-controlled TTLs, supervising the entry and exit of people. This was doubly important given the lack of a clear-cut spatial distinction of the liberated areas — there were no clear-cut limits between settler and guerilla territory. Naturally this idea should not be carried to extremes. Many TTLs in Victoria Province, such as Gutu and Bikita for example were effectively liberated areas. Security forces could not go into these areas except in large and heavily armed numbers. But a village could not be bombed and the crops destroyed just because it existed. Only in provinces to the north, where peasants had been driven into the strategic hamlets, called 'keeps', could people living outside of those be legitimately considered 'terrorist sympathisers'. Hence it was doubly important to create a political distinction of personnel between liberated areas and the rest. *Mujibas* knew the people living in the area and could automatically detect strangers who might be observed, questioned or even killed if suspicions were raised. They were intelligence as well as counter-intelligence agents, gathering information about the movements of security forces and discovering the presence of informers amongst the local population. Certain respected *mujibas* might carry a weapon, such as a grenade, and if an area

> was under attack they would fight alongside of the guerilla unit.
>
> But in addition to their security functions, the *mujibas* had many other important functions which highlight even more the special dual-power situation in Zimbabwe. Given the general absence of a distinctly separate economic system within the liberated areas ... the *mujibas* were amongst other things, the link between the guerillas and the colonial economy. They collected contributions from the people for the guerillas. These contributions took the form of money, food, medicines, drink, clothing ...
>
> The *mujibas* would [also] politicise the local population and help co-ordinate and organise the political meetings.[32]

Politicisation took largely the form of all-night *pungwes* (rallies). To judge by a ZANU-PF election meeting I attended in Selukwe TTL, where ZANLA had been very active during the war, these meetings were taken up largely with the chanting of slogans and singing of songs, in which the ZANU activists played the leading part. The message presented at this meeting was a radical one — the choice was between imperialism (Smith and Muzorewa) or socialism (ZANU-PF), the audience was told, but the role of the peasants was clearly meant to be a passive one, that of giving material and moral support to the party. It is interesting to note that the guerillas tended to encourage the observance of traditional African religion, even though in some parts of the country they established friendly, or at least neutral, relations with the local missionaries (the trial and deportation of the Catholic Bishop of Umtali, Donal Lamont, arose from such a situation). But:

> the traditional worship of *Mudzimu*, spirit mediums, was praised and promoted so that the guerillas whenever they go to a new area registered their presence and sought spiritual guidance. In addition they were given '*Bhute*' — special snuff which they sniffed in the course of their operations.[33]

Spirit mediums continue to play an important part in rural Shona society, claiming to serve as a bridge between the present generation and their ancestors and thereby both offering security and preserving kinship relations.[34] By linking their cause to the spirit mediums, the guerillas were able to stress the connection between their struggle and the *chimurenga* of 1896-97, in which mediums such as Nehanda were of great importance.

ZIPRA adopted very different tactics. The ZAPU guerillas were trained along conventional military lines by Cuban instructors in Angola. The eastern bloc provided them with sophisticated heavy weaponry. ZIPRA forces were committed only sparingly; in the field they were far more mobile than ZANLA and on the whole more prone to seek out and attack the security forces. Their relationship to the local population was also different. By the time ZIPRA guerillas were in the country on any scale, in 1976-77, a framework for the war had been set by the ZANLA offensive along the eastern border. ZAPU forces found themselves confined largely to areas where they had traditionally been strong — notably Matabeleland, but also Mashonaland West and parts of the Midlands. They tended to rely on the traditional party organisation (ZAPU remained, in one form or other, legal in 1975-78) and 'merely revitalised ZAPU structures without establishing an adminstrative network of committees and sub-committees. In other words, they did not systematise the political activities of the local population'. The study just quoted continues:

> To sustain high morale and enthusiastic support for ZAPU in the local population, the ZIPRA guerillas relied not on frequent 'base meetings' and slogans but on their military operations. Through their effective attacks on enemy installations and camps they generated a high degree of political affinity with the local peasants ...
>
> In the ZIPRA operational areas, many people talk about the guerillas as if they possess mystic power to demolish the enemy forces with ease. Having heard the bangs and seen 'security force trucks burning and soldiers dying and bleeding', the peasants regarded the guerillas as possessors of extraordinary power that had never been known before. Since the performers of this 'mystic power' had been sent to 'perform it' by Joshua Nkomo, his name also became associated with some inexplicable legend, 'possessing extra-ordinary power to conquer and liberate Zimbabwe'.[35]

Even though their command of the air and their superior firepower gave the regime an immense advantage, simple arithmetic suggested that time was not on the whites' side. They were outnumbered by blacks 25 to 1. By the end of the war the army numbered 20,000, including 14,000 mainly white conscripts, and elite units such as the all-white Rhodesia Light Infantry (1,000) and the Selous Scouts (1,800). Apart from this the regime could count on the paramilitary British South African Police (6,000), 35,000 police reservists (mainly white), and 6,000 guard force in the protected villages. The guerilla armies by the end of the war had little short of 40,000 men and women under arms, two-thirds ZANLA, one-third ZIPRA. These figures suggest a ratio of security forces to guerillas not especially favourable to the regime. The eventual extension of compulsory military service to all the white adult male population under 60 led to shortages of skilled manpower and contributed to the steady stream of whites out of the country (see Table 4). The pressure of increasing guerilla numbers forced the regime to rely increasingly on indiscriminate use of air attacks and on Fire Force, the helicopter-borne RLI. After the Pretoria agreement of September 1976, South Africa gave consistent material support to the regime, and the flow of supplies to Salisbury was increased by P.W. Botha when he became prime minister. The Huey helicopter gunships which the security forces somehow got hold of no doubt came via South Africa, who also supplied 'volunteers' to pilot the Fire Force helicopters. In June 1977 it was reported that there were 1,500 mercenaries, mainly from Britain and the US, serving in the security forces.[36] Many farmers also hired mercenaries to guard their property while they were away on military service (as late as February 1980, one election observer on the plane to Salisbury found himself sitting next to a Belgian ex-paratrooper who had served at Kolwezi in 1978 and was going out to protect a farm).

One remedy for the manpower shortage was to rely increasingly on black soldiers. By 1979 Africans made up 80 per cent of the regular army, mainly in the Rhodesian African Rifles, while the creation of the security force auxiliaries, recruited from supporters of the internal settlement parties, helped to relieve some of the pressure on the army and police. But this situation only served to re-inforce the truth that undiluted white power could not last indefinitely. On one estimate, ZANLA was by 1977 recruiting at the rate of 1,000 a month.[37] Cross-border raids into Mozambique continued, but even a devastating series of attacks on Chimoio and Tembue camps in November 1977, when some 1,200 guerillas were reported to have been killed, did not make a significant difference to the military situation. Lieutenant-General Peter Walls, Rhodesian commander of combined operations, argued that a political solution — i.e. some sort of deal with a section of the nationalists — was necessary to end the war.

Table 4: Net Migration of Europeans in Zimbabwe, 1970-79

Year	Net migration
1970	+6,331
1971	+9,407
1972	+8,825
1973	+1,682
1974	+ 580
1975	+1,928
1976	−7,072
1977	−10,908
1978	−13,709
1979	−9,557

Source: Zimbabwe Rhodesia Central Statistical Office, *Monthly Digest of Statistics*, February 1980, Table 1.

The Internal Settlement

It is in this context that the 'internal settlement' concluded on 3 March 1978 must be seen. Smith, once he had conceded the principle of majority rule, sought to establish it in a form as favourable to white interests as possible. Soon after the Geneva conference he told an audience of white businessmen: 'even if you believe that all nationalists are devils, you have only one choice: find the better of the devils'.[38] This was the rationale behind his post-Geneva policy of seeking an agreement with 'moderate' nationalists. Soured relations between Washington and Pretoria after the Carter administration came to office gave Smith a comparatively free hand. In September 1977 he dismissed the Anglo-American proposals for a settlement, which called for the disbanding of the Selous Scouts, RLI and other elite units and the integration of ZIPRA and ZANLA in the security forces, shortly after a meeting with the South African foreign minister, Pik Botha, who told the press: 'we are not going to let outsiders dictate to our part of the world'.[39]

The obvious candidate for the role of the 'better of the devils' was Biship Abel Muzorewa, excluded from the guerilla camps by the frontline presidents, squeezed out further by the formation of the Patriotic Front (although he had helped bring this re-alignment about by spurning feelers from Nkomo), yet whose United African National Council (UANC) enjoyed considerable popular support. When he returned to Salisbury in October 1976 100,000 people turned out to greet Muzorewa. Other nationalist politicians who had lost out in the post-detente manoeuvres rushed to the internal settlement banner — notably Ndabaningi Sithole and James Chikerema, while Chief Jeremiah Chirau, who had been appointed to the cabinet as window dressing in April 1976, launched the Zimbabwe United People's Organisation (ZUPO). Smith's personal preference, however, was for Joshua Nkomo who, despite ZIPRA's growing links with the eastern bloc, enjoyed the backing of both the British government and Tiny Rowlands of Lonrho. ZAPU was permitted to retain a legal organisation within the country until late 1978, while, by contrast, Canaan Banana's attempt to launch a legal front for ZANU, the People's Movement, was rapidly crushed.

Negotiations between ZAPU and representatives of the Salisbury regime, although encouraged by the British, Nigerian and Zambian governments, proved inconclusive and, after two secret meetings with Kaunda, Smith opened negotiations with Muzorewa, Sithole and Chirau in November 1977. The nationalists, as terrified of the guerillas as the settlers ('the men in the bush are not ours. We may be the first to face the firing squads', a ZUPO delegate said during the negotiations) gave Smith everything he asked for. The agreement eventually signed on 3 March 1978 promised elections based on universal suffrage by the end of the year, but set out a constitutional framework in which control of the army, police, judiciary and civil service would remain in white hands, while the settlers were given reserved seats in parliament and a veto over constitutional changes. In the meantime a transitional government was set up, presided over by an Executive Council consisting of Smith, Muzorewa, Sithole and Chirau, with black and white co-ministers in each department. As the speedy removal of Byron Hove, the UANC co-minister of justice, law and order, who had called for the Africanisation of the police and judiciary, showed, it was to be business as usual. Although a number of detainees were released and some protective villages closed down, the security forces continued to prosecute the war as ruthlessly as ever.[40]

Smith claimed that the internal settlement had destroyed 'any possibility of marxism ever taking over this country'.[41] Such hopes were based on the assumption that there was some truth in the claims of Muzorewa and Sithole that the bulk of the ZANLA guerillas supported them. But the call for a cease fire issued by the Executive Council at the beginning of May fell on stony ground. Some UANC and ZANU (Sithole) activists sent out to talk to the guerillas were killed. Meetings for Africans in support of the internal settlement were often complete failures. Ministers, including Chikerema, addressing a crowd of 2,500 in the Honde valley were shouted down. A meeting at Wankie was cancelled after only seven people turned up to hear three ministers, while three meetings in the Mtoko district were poorly attended — as a result, according to the district commissioner, of the 2,500 *mujibas* in the area.[42]

The war continued apace. Only three days after the 3 March agreement, the *Rhodesia Herald* reported that a dusk-to-dawn curfew had been imposed over a 70-kilometre belt of mainly white farming land to the north and east of Salisbury in an effort to create a buffer between the capital and Chinamore, Msana and Chikwakwa tribal trust lands, where ZANLA was active. At its nearest point the curfew area was only 20 kilometres from the city centre. In the far south of the country, the first protected village on the South African border was established, to embrace 20,000 Venda tribespeople 'subverted by terrorists'.[43] In April the Rhodesian Automobile Association advised motorists to travel in convoy.[44] In July and August there were gun battles with guerillas in the Salisbury townships of Highfield, Glen Norah and Mufakose, and in the centre of Gwelo. Several whites were killed by guerillas in the expensive white suburb of Borrowdale in northern Salisbury.[45] The rail link between Salisbury and Bulawayo was sabotaged twice. It was estimated that although some 3,500 ZANLA guerillas had been killed in 1976-78, their numbers in the east of the country had grown in that same period from 1,200 to more than 8,000.[46]

It was no doubt in part this grim military situation which led Smith to reconsider the possibility of a separate deal with Nkomo. They met in Lusaka on 14 August 1978. Although offered the chairmanship of the executive council, Nkomo insisted on holding a further meeting at which Mugabe and Muzorewa would be present. The ZANU leader, however, only learned of the secret contacts between Salisbury and Lusaka when he was summoned to Lagos and informed of the meeting by Brigadier Joseph Garba, the former Nigerian external affairs commissioner. Mugabe was furious and vetoed any further contacts with Salisbury, with the support of Nyerere and Machel, although not of Kaunda.[47] The affair brought to the surface tensions implicit in the Patriotic Front. ZANU had long resented Nkomo's failure to commit ZIPRA fully to the war, suspecting that the ZAPU guerillas' function was less to fight the regime than to serve as a counter-weight to ZANLA in the struggle to rule an independent Zimbabwe. On the ground there were clashes between the two wings of the PF. The old dividing line between ZANU and ZAPU spheres of influence, from east of Kariba to Beitbridge, was increasingly ignored — by June 1978 ZIPRA was within 20 miles of Salisbury and ZANLA only 20 miles from Bulawayo. Clashes between the guerillas were reported in the south-west and south-centre of the country and near Beitbridge.[48]

Then what Ian Smith called 'a stroke of fate' intervened to nullify his efforts to exploit these divisions and split the Patriotic Front. ZIPRA shot down an Air Rhodesia Viscount at Kariba on 3 September 1978. Forty passengers were killed in the crash or as they emerged from the wreckage. Smith was forced by the pressure of white opinion to slam the door on Nkomo, whom he described as a 'monster'. ZANU and ZAPU were banned and martial law imposed on 75 per cent of the country. In late September the security forces attacked 25 ZANLA bases in Mozambique. Elements of the FPLM (the Mozambican armed forces) in armoured personnel carriers led the resistance to the raids. But the worst was reserved for the ZAPU bases in Zambia, hitherto left alone as part of Smith's strategy of weaning Nkomo away from Mugabe. On 19 October a devastating raid on the ZIPRA camps at Chikumbi and near Mkushi left fifteen hundred guerillas dead. Further raids followed in November. Despite these measures, the military situation remained very serious. In December the guerillas blew up the central oil storage depot, destroying a quarter of the country's current stock. Another Viscount was shot down at Kariba in February 1979, the same month that Salisbury airport was mortared. Night seemed about to fall on white Rhodesia.

The Unlooked-for Peace

The break with Nkomo left Smith with no choice but to press ahead with the internal settlement, despite his growing contempt for Muzorewa. The new constitution published at the beginning of February 1979 created a hybrid 'Zimbabwe Rhodesia' whose elected black government would have the appearance but not the substance of power. Thus 28 out of the 100 seats in the House of Assembly were reserved for whites, less than one twenty-fifth of the population. The white MPs had a veto over constitutional changes affecting settler interests. White-dominated commissions controlled the security forces, courts and administration. It was a stooge constitution designed to conceal white rule behind a black puppet. The turnout in the elections under the new constitution, held between 17 and 22 April 1979, nonetheless surprised many observers — between 51 and 63 per cent of the overwhelmingly black electorate (depending on which estimate of the total population one accepts). Although this result could be explained by factors such as the activities of the auxiliaries in the TTLs and pressure by white farmers on their employees,[49] it was undoubtedly a blow for the PF, whose military capacity to deny the regime access to the countryside was shown to be less than it had claimed. Muzorewa's UANC won 51 out of the 72 African seats, and on 1 June the Bishop became prime minister, in name if not in fact.

The military situation had undoubtedly become more favourable to the regime. Rhodesian Canberras bombed a ZIPRA base at Luso in Angola on 26 February, a feat made possible only with South African help. Then the security forces struck at ZAPU headquarters in Lusaka on 13 April. The raids left ZIPRA in disarray, and there was a notable slowdown in infiltration across the north-western border from Botswana.[50] The security forces were deployed on a massive scale shortly before the April elections in a largely successful effort to counter a PF offensive aimed at disrupting the polls. The regime was greatly aided by the formation of the security force auxiliaries. The *Pfumo reVanhu* (Spear of the People), as they were called, numbered between 25,000 and 30,000 at their height, during the February 1980 elections. A few may have been guerillas who 'turned' and supported the UANC or ZANU (Sithole) after the 3 March agreement. Some were given training in African states which supported the internal settlement — Field Marshal Amin of Uganda was reported by Sithole's supporters to be 'very much behind' the 3 March agreement,[51] and there were reports that Libya had offered facilities to the UANC. The bulk of the *madzajutsaku*, however, were recruited from the unemployed youth of Zimbabwe. After the April elections they became effectively the UANC's armed wing — 183 auxiliaries supporting Sithole were killed on Muzorewa's orders. During the elections they were deployed massively around Salisbury and in 'fringe areas' such as Urungwe TTL where both ZANLA and ZIPRA were operating and the local population's allegiance uncertain.[52] In 1979 a new tactic was adopted with the specific aim of weakening the guerillas' hold on the peasantry. Operation Turkey amounted essentially to the creation of famine, especially in the liberated and semi-liberated areas (amounting to one third of the country according to ZANU).[53] In many tribal trust lands all grinding mills and shops were closed down in order to deny the guerillas access to food.

The international situation had also improved. On 16 October 1978 Kaunda re-opened the border between Rhodesia and Zambia. The Zambian economy was in a desperate state: in 1976-77 real per capita income fell from K198 to K185, while the number of wage earners declined from 393,000 in December 1975 to 373,000 in mid-1978. Low copper prices and transport difficulties (the Benguela railway to Lobito in Angola had been closed since the 1975-76 war, while the Tanzara railway linking the Copperbelt to Dar-es-salaam was still suffering from teething troubles) meant that Zambia was K500 million in arrears in payments for imports and profit and dividend remittances. Re-opening the border would enable Zambia to clear the 80,000 ton backlog of copper exports, 12 per cent of 1978 production. There could be no doubt that Kaunda was desperate for a settlement and that he could not afford to antagonise the western powers if they decided on one: the *Financial Mail* reported that 'Zambia requires substantial western assistance in the form of tolerance of existing debts and fresh grants and loans'.[54]

The west itself appeared to be swinging right. In October 1978 the Carter administration had been forced by the pro-Rhodesian lobby in Congress to allow Smith and Muzorewa to tour the US. The following May the Senate in Washington voted by 75 to 19 that the Rhodesian elections had been free, that Salisbury had satisfied the demand for black majority rule and that sanctions should be lifted. Best of all, a new Tory government took office in London on 4 May 1979. A Conservative Party team of observers had already declared the Rhodesian elections to be 'free and fair'. Accordingly Margaret Thatcher told a press conference in Canberra on 2 July that economic sanctions against Rhodesia could not be renewed in November. Recognition of the Muzorewa regime — whether open or stealthy — seemed inevitable.

That this did not come to pass can be explained in one word: Nigeria. The military regime in Lagos had already adopted a policy designed to reduce foreign capital's hold on the economy. This and austerity measures taken after the real price of oil fell in 1975-78 hit British firms especially hard. British exports to Nigeria, the UK's most important market outside Europe and North America, fell from £1,133.37 million in 1978 to £638.24 million the following year.[55] Unilever's United Africa Company, accustomed to a 40 per cent rate of return on capital invested in Nigeria, saw its profits halved in the year ending 30 September 1979.[56] And then Lagos began to tighten the screws. Within a few months of Thatcher's and Muzorewa's election victories the Nigerian government nationalised BP's assets, withdrew its deposits from the local associate of Barclays Bank and banned British companies' bids for federal contracts. The final blow was the takeover of BP, denying the company the right to 12 million tons of crude oil at a time when spot prices were going through the ceiling. It was announced on 31 July 1979 just before the Commonwealth Conference was due to open in Lusaka. The message had already got through. A few weeks earlier a delegation of British firms with interests in Nigeria, including BP, Dunlop and Barclays International, went to Whitehall to beg the new government not to recognise Muzorewa.

Their pleas found a ready hearing at the Foreign and Commonwealth Office, where the new Secretary of State was Lord Carrington, who had on taking office resigned a directorship in Rio Tinto Zinc, a company with considerable mining interests throughout southern Africa. Carrington and his senior civil servants did not wish to antagonise Nigeria further — already Thatcher's support for Muzorewa had cost British firms some £250 millions in lost contracts.[57] They were also worried that if the war went on it would end in a confrontation between the frontline states, backed by Russia and Cuba, and South Africa. They were able to persuade Thatcher to give the old Anglo-American proposals for a deal involving both Salisbury and the PF one more try. (American pressure may have helped — in June Carter announced that sanctions would stay in force.) This change in policy was signalled in a reply Thatcher gave to a question in the House of Commons on 25 July, a few days before she flew to Lusaka.[58] At the conference she proposed an all-party conference chaired by Britain. Eating her earlier praise of the internal settlement, she even criticised some of the more blatantly racist aspects of the constitution. The result of this first U-turn by the Tory government was the Lancaster House conference, which opened in London on 10 September 1979.

Muzorewa and Smith agreed only reluctantly to participate in the conference. That they did so at all reflected the basic difficulties the regime found itself in, despite some improvements in the situation since the nadir reached at the end of 1978. Most important was the state of the economy. Sanctions imposed after UDI led to a boom stimulated by import-substitution — in 1968-74 real gross domestic product rose at an annual rate of 8.6 per cent. After 1974 the world recession and the war together caused a steep economic decline — real gross domestic product fell 13.5 per cent between 1974 and 1979.[59] The resulting fall in per capita income (see Table 5) was felt most severely by Africans. They also bore the brunt of mass unemployment, which rose even during the boom. Every year between 1976 and 1978, 178,000 black schoolchildren left school, while only 20,000 new jobs were created each year.[60] Unemployed youths provided the guerillas and *mujibas* — and the auxiliaries — with their recruits. The burden of the war drained the economy — defence spending rose by 610 per cent in 1971-78, from 2.6 per cent of gross national product in 1975 to 7.7 per cent three years later[61] — and forced the regime to go increasingly into debt. British officials were told after the December 1979 agreement that Rhodesia had borrowed Z$800 million from South Africa in 1978-80 to finance current expenditure.[62] Without the access to western loans and markets that only international recognition could bring, further economic decline was inevitable.

Table 5: The Zimbabwean Economy, 1970-79

Year	GDP Constant 1965 prices	Inflation	GDP per head Constant 1965 prices
	percentage per year		Zimbabwean dollars
1970	3.8	3.5	185
1971	12.0	3.2	200
1972	9.6	4.0	211
1973	3.2	6.0	211
1974	9.3	9.8	223
1975	−1.1	9.5	213
1976	−1.6	9.5	203
1977	−7.3	9.5	182
1978	−3.0	9.0	171
1979	−0.9	11.0	163

Source: *Financial Times* Survey on Zimbabwe, 22 April 1980

Throughout the second half of 1979 the regime sought to keep up the military pressure. Within hours of taking office Muzorewa approved a cross-border raid. On 26 June ZIPRA headquarters in Lusaka and the nearby guerilla camp at Chikumbi were attacked. Raids on Zambia and Mozambique in October and November seemed designed to shatter those countries' infrastructures. In order to put further pressure on Kaunda, Salisbury cut off Zambia's supply of maize from

South Africa in early November. The raiders did not always have things their own way. When Rhodesian forces stormed into Mozambique on 5 September they found themselves faced at Chokwe in the Limpopo valley with well-dug-in ZANLA and FPLM troops backed up by T-55 tanks. A Huey helicopter was shot down and crack RLI troops mutinied when ordered to make a suicidal frontal attack on the ZANLA/FPLM positions (some of the mutineers were still in gaol at the time of the February elections). Time was not on the regime's side.

The negotiations at Lancaster House were lengthy and acrimonious. Carrington, who chaired the conference, adopted what seemed to be brinkmanship tactics. He first forced the Salisbury delegation to drop some of the worst features of the constitution — the white-dominated commissions which controlled the state machine, for example — and to accept reduced white representation in parliament. Then it was the Patriotic Front's turn. After a series of ultimatums from Carrington, who adjourned the conference indefinitely on 11 October when he didn't get the answer he wanted, Nkomo and Mugabe agreed to a draft which gave whites 20 out of the 100 seats in the House of Assembly and a veto over constitutional changes; they also accepted a clause which guaranteed to the owners of property compulsorily acquired by the state 'adequate compensation'[63] in exchange for a vague promise of Anglo-American aid to buy out the white farmers. The same process was repeated in the case of, first, the arrangements for the transition to majority rule — a British Governor backed up by a predominantly British Commonwealth Monitoring Force would take charge for the two-month period before elections were held — and, second, for the ceasefire — the guerillas would gather in 15 assembly points well away from the urban areas supervised by the British while the Rhodesian army withdrew to barracks and South African troops pulled out of the country. In each case the British proposals were accepted speedily by Muzorewa, only reluctantly and after the breakdown of the conference seemed inevitable by the Patriotic Front.

It all seemed as if British diplomacy had wrought a miracle. In reality Carrington was playing with loaded dice. Not only did he enjoy the unusual advantage of knowing precisely what the PF would propose, since he had their hotels and offices bugged,[64] but he had the frontline states firmly on his side. Not only was Zambia desperate for a settlement: the role played by President Samora Machel of Mozambique was essential to Carrington's success. The Mozambican regime was in late 1979 moving towards much closer relations with the west, and was eager to end the Zimbabwean war, which had cost the country's economy dear. In 1978 the United Nations estimated that the closure of the Rhodesia border meant a loss of between $108 and $134 million. Rhodesian attacks caused $44 million worth of damage, while Mozambique had to support 150,000 Zimbabwean refugees.[65] One source close to the ZANU leadership declared: 'I have little doubt that if they had not been faced with unendurable pressure from Mozambique the old guard of ZANU-PF would not have entered into the Lancaster House negotiations, nor have come to the terms which they did.'[66] As it was, Carrington was able to issue his ultimatums secure in the knowledge that, sooner or later, Machel, Nyerere and Kaunda would bludgeon the Patriotic Front leaders into line.

The cease-fire agreement was eventually signed on 21 December 1979, ending seven years of war. Only minor concessions had been made by the British — chiefly the addition of another assembly point in the Midlands — but the frontline presidents left Nkomo and Mugabe no choice. Machel's personal intervention stopped the PF leaders flying to New York to denounce Carrington at the UN and forced them to accept the British proposals on 17 December. By that time Muzorewa had already gone home to start his election campaign and the country had reverted to the status of a British colony. Lord Soames, the Tory cabinet minister appointed Governor of Southern Rhodesia, had arrived in Salisbury on 12 December. The trap, it seemed, had been set. It only remained for ZANU and ZAPU to walk into it.

3. The Ambiguous Victory

'In all revolutions it's the masses who lose out', I was told by a Salisbury investment consultant in February 1980. 'We need a strong and ruthless government in Zimbabwe today to hold down the workers and peasants. Only Mugabe and Nkomo are capable of providing such a government. I expect the Patriotic Front to win the elections and that will be the best result in the circumstances.' In line with this cynical but remarkably accurate judgement, the Anglo-American Corporation (for a subsidiary of which the person quoted works) is reported to have contributed money not only to Muzorewa's election campaign but also to those of both wings of the Patriotic Front! For, as surprising as ZANU-PF's landslide victory in the election was the rapidity with which the Mugabe government sought to provide Anglo-American and other foreign companies with the security they needed in order to continue to exploit Zimbabwe's people and natural resources. In this chapter we shall try to describe and account for both these developments.

The Counter-Revolution That Failed

The strategy pursued by Lord Soames and the other British officials dispatched to preside over the Zimbabwean elections represented a continuation of long-standing British strategy — to wean Nkomo away from his alliance with ZANU and into collaboration with Smith and Muzorewa. They were aided by ZANU's decision to run its own candidates in the elections rather than stand on a joint slate with ZAPU. (The main advocate of the latter policy, Josiah Tongogara, died in a car accident in Mozambique in December 1979.) British calculations were based on the assumption that no single party would win a majority in the House of Assembly — a reasonable expectation, it seemed, since, with 20 seats reserved for whites, a party would have to win nearly two-thirds of the African vote to capture 51 out of the remaining 80 seats. In the absence of such a majority, Soames hoped to construct a coalition embracing ZAPU and the UANC with perhaps the support of the Rhodesian Front, which won all 20 white seats in a separate election, from the backbenches. Plans were drawn up for a military strike on ZANLA forces in the assembly camps to neutralise the uprising which would almost inevitably follow the formation of a Nkomo-Muzorewa government.[1] Nkomo, it should be noted, refused to rule out any possible government combination: 'Coalitions come about when you fail to get a sufficient number', he told a press conference in Gwelo on 24 February. 'You wait until the time comes and then you decide.'[2] ZAPU adopted the name Patriotic Front to capitalise on an image of unity.

Within the framework of this strategy, the British permitted the existing administration to operate much as it had in the past. ZANU-PF (as it now called itself to mark itself off from Sithole's rump ZANU) was subject to constant harassment by the state apparatus — some 3,000 party campaign workers were arrested including a number of candidates. A campaign of dirty tricks, apparently mounted by elements within the security forces, included several attempts on Mugabe's life, a bombing campaign against Salisbury churches (in the hope of smearing ZANU-PF as anti-Christian), a fake issue, attacking Mugabe, of the Catholic weekly, *Moto*, the only paper to support ZANU-PF, and an explosion which destroyed the Gwelo offices of *Moto*'s publishers, Mambo Press. Most serious of all was the deployment of the auxiliaries, despite their openly partisan role. Major Nick Fawcett of the RLI told reporters on 23 January that 'the auxiliaries' job was to counter the guerillas' socialist ideology and to implant the counter-ideology of Zimbabweanism based on nationalism, democracy, peace and livelihood.'[3] They were dispatched to rural areas where ZANLA had been most active and attempted, with great brutality, to break the peasants' allegiance to ZANU-PF. They were joined by UANC activists, many of them unemployed young thugs from the townships. Finally, and in violation of the Lancaster House agreement which provided that 'the task of maintaining law and order in the pre-independence period will be the responsibility of the civil police',[4] the biggest ever call-up of white national servicemen took place during the election period, to protect the voters against ZANU-PF 'intimidation', the British claimed.[5]

Muzorewa ran a lavish campaign (according to the Organisation of African Unity he received $55 million from South Africa) centred on the theme of anti-communism. 'This is what communism means. Death. Oppression. Suffering. Poverty. Starvation. Human Misery', ran a not untypical piece of UANC propaganda. The same theme was pushed by the supposedly neutral forces of the state. An unusually friendly and talkative group of white national servicemen belonging to the Police Anti-Terrorist Unit in Seki TTL on the outskirts of Salisbury freely admitted that they had distributed leaflets warning voters to reject socialism and communism (although, as one of them admitted with unconscious candour, 'as the Africans own the land collectively, they practise communism in their everyday lives, don't they?').[6] The team of official Commonwealth observers was told of a meeting of police reservists in Salisbury where it was stressed that the task was to keep ZANU-PF out and get the Bishop in.

'Of all the nine parties contesting the election ZANU is the only one that has a socialist programme', Nathan Shamuyarira said the day before the election.[7] And indeed the party's election manifesto stated clearly that:

> ZANU's ideological belief is SOCIALISM. We believe that the achievement of political power by the People will remain hollow in terms of their material development unless it can translate itself into quantitative and qualitative benefits from the economy. Such a translation of political power must necessarily be by way of economic power in social form. ZANU thus believes in the development of a *socialist economy*.

Certainly ZANU-PF on the stump stressed that the choice in the election was one between socialism and capitalism. The election meeting I attended in Selukwe TTL on 21 February included this exchange between ZANU-PF speaker and peasant audience:

> — What does majority rule means?
> — A full belly!

(The meeting, at a school in the middle of nowhere, was also attended by a dozen white national servicemen in a mine-proofed troop carrier — to protect it against ZIPRA, they claimed — and a police informer who took down everything the speakers said. This was what 'intimidation' meant for the mass of the population.)

But the meeting reflected the degree to which ZANU-PF was a multi-class alliance. The main speaker was S.E. Matiyenga, an accountant in Gwelo. The local party chairman, T. Gandire, was a fat little man who owned a second-hand American car and wore braces. He had owned the hotel at Donga, a township in Selukwe TTL, but now had a couple of stores and lived in fear of his life after threats made against him by a white rancher who ran the local auxiliaries. Then there was the charming and urbane African writer and businessman I met later in Salisbury. He had just returned to Zimbabwe after many years in exile to set up an import-export business and join the local board of Barclays Bank. He made his support for Mugabe quite obvious.

The dense popular organisation which ZANU-PF had built up during the war and which was revealed at meetings such as the one I attended lay behind the election results: 2.7 million Africans, 94 per cent of the electorate, voted between 27 and 29 February. The outcome of the poll, announced on 4 March, was a landslide victory for ZANU-PF, which won 57 seats — more than enough to form a government on its own. The UANC, paying the price for its role in the internal settlement, was obliterated, while the PF was reduced to the status of an Ndebele party, winning almost all its seats in the two provinces of Matabeleland (Table 6). 'The groundwork [for ZANU-PF's triumph] had been laid long before the very brief campaign period', Lionel Cliffe writes. People told him: 'It didn't matter if there were no campaign meetings in our area, we had been going to politicisation meetings (*pungwe*) at night for years'.[8] As another perceptive observer noted on the eve of the poll after attending a ZANU-PF rally in Gutu TTL (Victoria province), where some of the most bitter fighting had occurred:

> For the peasant supporters of ZANU, as much as for Ian Smith's Rhodesian Front, this week's election is nothing but a continuation of a war which began with the settlers' arrival in 1890 ... The elections this week are seen only as the latest phase in it, a celebration — so the people here

hope — of the military victory they have won.[9]

The brilliant choice of a cock as the party's symbol was apparently 'made by the spirit mediums and then adopted by the party',[10] enabling ZANU-PF once again to stress the continuity of the struggles — from the first *chimurenga* in the 1890s, to the second waged by ZANLA 80 years later.

Only in Matabeleland did this appeal fail. While the PF's national campaign, stressing peace and reconciliation, and centred on the person of Nkomo — 'Father Zimbabwe' as the posters described him — failed, it preserved a solid popular base among the Ndebele.[11] Even in Matabeleland South, where ZANLA had operated in about a third of the province during the war, the people backed PF. The local peasantry, although drawn into the standard ZANU structures of committees, *mujibas* and *pungwes*, were infuriated by the guerillas' slogan of *'Pasi naNkomo'* - 'Down with Nkomo' - and called them contemptuously the *'O-pasi'*, 'the down-withs'. Even during the elections, they would attend ZANU-PF rallies and hold their own secret meetings to organise the PF vote. Nkomo was careful to present himself as the heir of the Ndebele kings — one of his biggest rallies in Matabeleland was at Njelele mountain, an important spiritual centre for the Ndebele, when a quarter of a million people attended.

Table 6: The Zimbabwe Elections, 27-29 February 1980

Party	Votes	Total Vote percentages	Seats
PF (ZAPU)	638,879	24.113	20
UANC	219,307	8.277	3
ZANU-PF	1,668,992	62.992	57

Source: *The Times*, 5 March 1980.

Nevertheless, the plans for a Muzorewa/Smith/Nkomo coalition collapsed like a pack of cards with the news of ZANU-PF's victory. When Walls approached the British shortly after voting had closed and asked them to declare the election null and void on the grounds of ZANU-PF 'intimidation' (the standard white Rhodesian explanation of nationalist popular support), he was given the brush-off, as he later complained. The angry General, still in control of the security forces, could have implemented Operation Quartz, the British-approved plans for a strike on the guerilla camps, on his own, but only with the support of Pretoria. It seems likely that Piet Botha, like Margaret Thatcher, did not have the stomach for the sort of international row a white coup would have provoked. Lord Soames, in line with a Whitehall decision to make the best of a bad job, speedily switched horses, and set out with all the traditional skills of British diplomacy to woo Mugabe — with remarkable success.

The Revolution That Never Was

On the evening of 3 March 1980, two years to the day since the internal settlement whose purpose was to prevent this moment ever happening, Robert Mugabe addressed the nation. Although the results were announced the next morning, it was clear that he had won. Mugabe appealed for calm and respect for law and order. The next day, installed by Soames as Prime-Minister-designate, he appeared on television again to promise no victimisations, no nationalisations, respect for the constitution, national reconciliation. He asked General Walls to preside over the integration of ZANLA and ZIPRA with the security forces. *The Times* found itself praising Mugabe's 'considerable if perhaps calculated generosity' and reflected that 'the British government has rather unexpectedly got what it always said it wanted — the basis for a stable Zimbabwe in which the white population could stay and help.'[12]

Indeed, from his return to Zimbabwe on 27 January Mugabe had gone out of his way to moderate ZANU-PF's radicalism. The party manifesto contained a number of specific proposals — resettlement of peasants on unused or abandoned land, under-utilised land and land owned by absentees; state partnership in the mining industry; compulsory free primary and secondary education; a free national health service. All these were significant reforms, but they did not add up to the 'socialist transformation of Zimbabwean society' the manifesto promised. After the declaration that 'ZANU's ideological belief is SOCIALISM' came a qualifying clause:

> In working towards the socialist transformation of Zimbabwean society, a ZANU government will, nevertheless,

> recognise historical, social and other existing practical realities of Zimbabwe. One of these existing practical realities is the capitalist system which cannot be transformed overnight. Hence, while a socialist transformation process will be brought underway in many areas of the existing economic sectors, it is recognised that private enterprise will have to continue until circumstances are ripe for socialist change.

There were other signs of moderation. At a huge rally at Fort Victoria on 10 February, Mugabe said: '*Pamperi neBSAP!*' — 'Forward with the British South Africa Police!' It is normal for the crowd at a Zimbabwean political meeting to repeat the slogans shouted by the speakers; this time, however, the people refused to do so, even though Mugabe repeated the slogan several times. He also declared that 'we will carry on trade with South Africa' and 'not engage ourselves directly in the struggle in South Africa'.[13] According to Nicholas Ashford, the well-informed *Times* correspondent in southern Africa:

> Mr Mugabe's recently found pragmatism derives in large part from President Machel of Mozambique ... President Machel, whose own country has suffered severely as a result of the Rhodesian war, was largely responsible for Mr Mugabe's decision to go through with the Lancaster House agreement.
>
> He has subsequently emphasised to Mr Mugabe the need to avoid any actions which could lead to an early white exodus or renewed conflict between rival black factions. He pointed out the dangers of an internal white coup or intervention by South Africa should Mr Mugabe try to move too fast.[14]

In line with this strategy of re-assuring both the settlers and foreign investors, two whites were included in the cabinet announced on 11 March. They were David Smith, leader of the 'moderate' wing of the Rhodesian Front, and Dennis Norman, president of the white Commercial Farmers Union, appointed respectively Minister of Commerce and Industry and Minister of Agriculture. As promised, a coalition with PF had been formed, although ZANU-PF's partners had to content themselves with scraps. Nkomo was given the home affairs portfolio, to which was added control of the police. However, Mugabe reserved responsibility for security and defence for himself, and control of the district commissioners who run rural Zimbabwe was transferred from home affairs to Edson Zvobgo, ZANU-PF Minister of Local Government. Three PF veterans were given relatively minor portfolios, while the lion's share of the posts went to members of the ZANU-PF central committee. Only one guerilla, however, was included — Teurai Ropa Nhongo, former commander of Chimoio camp and wife of ZANLA Commander-in-Chief Rex Nhongo. The titular post of President was given to Canaan Banana, a Kalanga and one of ZANU-PF's few prominent figures in Matabeleland, Nkomo's stronghold. Bernard Chidzero, a UN technocrat who had advised both Nkomo and Muzorewa's delegations at Geneva, was appointed Minister of Economic Planning.

In late March there was a wave of strikes as black workers strove to translate the political victory into economic improvements. Some 16,000 workers were involved in the first outburst, in five industrial centres — Salisbury, Bulawayo, Gwelo, Gatooma, Umtali. Among the 41 workplaces hit were Danby Mine (1,500 workers), Cone Textile (900), Bata Shoes (900), and David Whitehead, a textile company owned by Lonrho. The strikes put the ZANU-PF left in the firing line. Kumbirai Kangai, Minister-designate of Labour, who had been briefly detained in 1978 for his association with the 'marxist-leninists' Hamadziripi and Gumbo, said that 'discipline at work must remain part and parcel of the freedom we have attained.' Maurice Nyagumbo, Minister-designate of Mines, a former member of the South African Communist Party, declared that 'we never promised instant pay increases. We said that the only way to get results was by working hard.'[15] Kangai insisted that the strikers observe existing procedures — principally the Industrial Conciliation Act, originally passed in 1934 under pressure from white workers to exclude blacks from skilled jobs. One study points out that its provisions 'restrict the freedom and limit the powers of the trade unions. The most important restriction is the lack of any real right to strike' because of the system of voluntary and compulsory arbitration modelled on South African legislation. A 1971 amendment authorises the government to ban strikes which it believes 'would prejudice the public interest'.[16]

Kangai and his deputy were able to get the strikers back to work with a mixture of threats and promises, but in early May a new strike wave shook some of the biggest enterprises in the country — 9,000 came out at Hippo Valley Estates and 8,000 at Triangle Estates, two sugar plantations in the south-eastern Lowveld owned by South African multinationals, respectively Anglo-American and Hulletts Corporation, and 4,000 at Wankie Colliery, another Anglo-American subsidiary. Once again Kangai went into action. After persuading the Hippo Valley strikers to return to work, he said: 'I myself told them that the government is opposed to strike action and that they should negotiate through proper industrial channels'.[17] The strike wave, which spread to a number of smaller factories, prompted Mugabe to threaten that 'corrective measures' would be used against workers.[18] An increased minimum wage was announced after some delay at the end of May — from 1 July workers in commerce and industry would get a minimum of Z$70 a month, in mining Z$43 (plus Z$27 in kind) and in agriculture and domestic service Z$30.[19] Although this meant a 50 per cent rise for farm workers, it was a slap in the face for urban industrial workers. As the *Financial Times* pointed out, 'not only is Z$70 below the Poverty Datum Line figure calculated nine months ago by the University of Zimbabwe, which was over Z$100 a month. It was also well below what the workers themselves had been anticipating.'[20]

ZANU-PF's response to the strikes was in line with Mugabe's overall strategy. There are three issues which are fundamental to the nature of a future Zimbabwe — land, foreign investment and relations with South Africa. In each case the new government sought to accept, and modify gradually, the existing structures. As we saw in chapter two, the basis of white power in Rhodesia lay in the settlers' monopoly of the best land and the low-wage economy which resulted. While the ZANU-PF election manifesto promised land resettlement and the encouragement of collective agriculture, it also stated that 'the private sector will be retained but restricted only to efficient farmers.' Almost by definition, since the land system after 1890 was organised to systematically favour the whites, it is the latter who are the efficient farmers.

In 1976 European output accounted for 76 per cent of total agricultural output and 92 per cent of marketed produce (much of African agricultural production goes to meet subsistence needs and therefore is not sold on the market).[21] Furthermore, production within the European sector is highly concentrated — over half of white output comes from 10 to 12 per cent of the farms.[22] Multinational companies play an important role in various branches of agriculture — for example, cattle ranching (Liebig and Lonrho), sugar and citrus estates (Anglo-American and Hulletts). A majority of white farms are too inefficient to survive without state subsidy — some 60 per cent of them did not pay any income tax since 1976, while Z$138.2 million were paid out by the state to white farmers in 1977-79.[23] Mechanisation and the growing capital-intensity of agricultural production have led some of the big plantations (notably Triangle and Hippo Valley) away from a reliance on unskilled foreign contract labour towards a policy designed to create a more skilled and stable workforce.[24]

A land reform which left the efficient farms alone would not affect the big ranches and plantations, which in any case could quite easily absorb the rise in labour-costs caused by an increased minimum wage. The smaller and less efficient white farms could be taken over without a significant fall in agricultural production. The chief constraint would be the cost (over Z$500 million to buy 75 per cent of white land at current prices).[25] ZANU-PF's 'socialist' land policy would then seem rather similar to that implemented in 'capitalist' Kenya after independence, when the big foreign-owned plantations were left alone, and the inefficient, state-subsidised mixed European farms taken over and transferred to what rapidly became a black kulak class.[26]

A similar strategy has been pursued in relation to foreign investment. Asked about the private sector and the multinationals Mugabe replied: 'I'll leave things as they are'.[27] 'Things as they are' were summed up in a study published shortly after ZANU-PF's election victory:

> It is hard to find a sub-Saharan African example comparable to the Zimbabwean case in which the role of foreign capital has been so long established, so deeply integrated in the sectors producing the bulk of output, so strongly interconnected with local capital.

Total foreign investment rose some 300 per cent between 1963 and 1978-79, from £350 million to £1,230-1,640 million, amounting to 67-73 per cent of the total capital stock. The main foreign investors were Britain (50 per cent) and South Africa (30 per cent). In some sector's foreign capital's domination is complete. Thus in 1974, 14 mines accounted for 73 per cent of all mining output. All but one or two were operated by foreign companies.[28] Mineral exports in 1979 were valued at over Z$200 million, about a third of total exports.[29] In banking Barclays, Standard Chartered, Grindlays and Nedbank hold unrivalled sway, while the multinationals are almost as dominant in other sectors — manufacture, agriculture, hotels.

Mugabe went out of his way to re-assure foreign investors. Opening the Bulawayo International Trade Fair on 5 May 1980 he made a mild speech in which he said: 'We welcome investment, but it must be Zimbabwe orientated.'[30] The ensuing uproar over the suggestion that some profits should not be repatriated abroad had Mugabe assuring the annual general meeting of the Chamber of Mines, the most powerful group of capitalists in the country, within 48 hours that 'it is not my government's intention to legislate against the repatriation of profits'. He denied that the government planned to take a 35 per cent stake in the mining industry or to set up workers' committees in the mines.[31] He also arranged to work to meet Harry Oppenheimer, head of the Anglo-American empire.[32] Moreover, the new government steered its foreign policy towards the west. Simon Muzenda, the foreign minister, explained that 'we will be very close to our former colonisers'.[33] Zimbabwe's first diplomatic missions were in London, Washington and Addis Ababa (capital of the OAU). In September 1980 Mugabe visited Washington to plead for increased western aid.

Equal moderation was pursued in relation to South Africa. Mugabe, as we have seen, even before the elections ruled out the use of Zimbabwe for military action against South Africa. On taking office he declared: 'We would want South Africa to regard us as a good neighbour, in the same way we intend to regard her as a good neighbour.'[34] This policy was dictated in part by economic necessity — 90 per cent of Zimbabwe's import-export traffic went via South African transport routes, while in 1979 South Africa bought about a quarter of Zimbabwe's exports and provided 30-40 per cent of her imports[35] — and in part by the understandable desire not to provoke war by a powerful neighbour after seven years of bloody internal conflict (even after South African troops were withdrawn from Zimbabwean soil, a large portion of Pretoria's regular army was concentrated across the Limpopo in the northern Transvaal). But 'good neighbourliness' went a little further than that. In April 1980 the *Financial Mail* reported that 'in a significant diplomatic move on the eve of Zimbabwean independence, Pretoria and Salisbury have tacitly agreed to maintain trade links in terms of the Preferential Trade Agreement signed in 1964'.[36] That the South African regime should agree to such a move when it was under heavy pressure from the clothing, textile, footwear and domestic appliance industries to close the border to cheap Zimbabwean imports was a sign that Botha was ready to play with Mugabe.

Relations subsequently deteriorated, but Mugabe did not take any economic measures against South Africa, nor did he change his policy on guerilla bases. In August 1980 he met the president of the South African ANC, Oliver Tambo, who said afterwards that he planned to open an office in Salisbury, but that he accepted Mugabe's ban on any armed actions against South Africa from Zimbabwean soil.[37]

In the short term, Mugabe sought to balance between two conflicting aims: on the one hand, to secure control of the state machine; on the other, to prevent the massive outflow of settlers that had proved so economically disruptive in Mozambique. He was reasonably successful in preventing a drastic collapse in white morale — indeed, his broadcasts on 3 and 4 March created a temporary wave of euphoria among the whites. Between January and April 1980 4,222 people emigrated from Zimbabwe and 1,585 settled there; the comparable figures for the same period in 1979 were 5,322 and 1,266.[38]

The price of this policy was to abandon any attempt radically to restructure the state apparatus. A couple of months after independence Nicholas Ashford reported in *The Times*:

> Perhaps what is most striking of all is that apart from the new faces in government so many other people at the top remain the same — for the time being at least. Lieutenant-General Peter Walls, for example, the man who directed the Rhodesian security forces against Mr Mugabe's guerillas in Mozambique, is now in overall charge not only of his own forces but the guerilla armies as well. Then

> there is Mr George Smith, the man who drew up the 1969 [apartheid] constitution, who has retained his position as Secretary to the cabinet. Mr David Young, who as Permanent Secretary at the Treasury masterminded Zimbabwe's remarkable economic drive to overcome the effect of sanctions, remains at the Treasury. And Mr Ken Flower, formerly Mr Ian Smith's spy chief, is now Mr Mugabe's head of intelligence.[39]

The most urgent task Mugabe found himself grappling with was that of the armed forces. Before the election ZANU-PF's policy was essentially to dissolve the security forces, amalgamating the acceptable elements into a new army formed out of ZIPRA and ZANLA. But as part of the policy of conciliation, the process was reversed — the guerillas were integrated into the security forces under British supervision. It was hoped that by the end of 1980 10,000 out of the 35,000 guerillas in the camps would have been assimilated into the regular forces. The problem lay in what to do with the rest of them, increasingly fed up with the makeshift camps, unwilling to give up their arms, doubtful of their chances of civilian employment, impatient about the slow pace of change, suspicious of their party rivals. Troops and police had to be deployed to deal with 'dissident' guerillas belonging to both ZANLA and ZIPRA. Conflicts between ZANU-PF and PF themselves exacerbated the situation — elements within the former demanded exclusive power for their party, while Nkomo, backed by a formidable military wing, was unhappy about PF's subordinate position within the government. Then Edgar Tekere, Secretary-General of ZANU-PF and Minister of Manpower, was arrested for the murder of a white farmer in August 1980. The affair threatened to polarise ZANU-PF between 'moderates' such as Mugabe and Muzenda and 'radicals' such as Tekere who had a large following among the guerillas and had only shortly before his arrest threatened to crush Nkomo.

There were also signs that, quite simply, power had begun to corrupt ZANU-PF. According to one report:

> Profligate spending on luxury homes, cars and foreign travel is beginning to raise eyebrows both in Salisbury and abroad. Public records show that Mugabe's ruling party

> has spent $1.4 million buying houses for senior functionaries. Treasury sources say the government owes Air Zimbabwe $3.3 million for such public relations exercises as sending 70 representatives to Tito's funeral in Yugoslavia; 40 junketeers accompanied President Canaan Banana on a state visit in Romania; 45 friends and aids went with Mugabe to the United States.[40]

Reform or Revolution?

Rosa Luxemburg wrote in 1899:

> People who pronounce themselves in favour of the method of legislative reform *in place of and in contradistinction to* the conquest of political power and social revolution, do not really choose a more tranquil, calmer and slower road to the *same* goal, but a *different* goal. Instead of taking a stand for the establishment of a new society they take a stand for the surface modification of the old society.[41]

These words seemed to apply directly to Zimbabwe 80 years later, where Robert Mugabe adopted 'the method of legislative reform' rather than that of 'social revolution'.

Two arguments could be made in his defence. The first was that ZANU-PF was still on the road to 'the establishment of a new society' — it was simply longer and more difficult than had previously been thought. Thus Kumbirai Kangai told an interviewer after the election:

> The goals we were fighting for have not been abandoned ... We believe we are going through a national-democratic revolution whereby the institutions, the society has to be democratised. This is a national democratic phase but it is also a transition to socialism.[42]

The language was that of Stalin, via Mao — that of 'uninterrupted revolution by stages': first, the national-democratic stage, then the socialist one. But in Zimbabwe no such clear demarcation could be made. The white monopoly of political power was merely the crystallisation of a web of social relations involving, crucially, land, cheap labour and foreign capital. Without the expropriation of the big plantations and other multinational interests 'national democracy' in Zimbabwe would be meaningless.

The second argument was simply the pressure of circumstances. At each stage one could point to external factors — Machel's intervention during Lancaster House, the fear of war with South Africa after the elections — that forced Mugabe to compromise. There is some force in this argument — only a fool would have demanded that ZANU-PF provoke a South African invasion after the bloodletting of the previous seven years. But it is less a matter of individual tactical choices than of the overall strategy of which they were part. From the beginning Mugabe placed his hopes on a guerilla army based in Mozambique. This choice forced him into dependence upon Machel and the other frontline leaders, a dependence which lead to the Lancaster House agreement and ZANU-PF's moderation from January 1980 onwards.

Was there an alternative? We believe there was. Mugabe could have based his strategy instead on the development of a mass movement of workers and peasants. As it was, the Zimbabwean masses were called on to participate within ZANU structures under the party's leadership. Their role was an essentially passive one — of support for the guerillas and the central committee. The possibility of the masses acting on their own and developing their own independent organisations within which different parties could contend for leadership was not envisaged. The model of socialism adopted by ZANU-PF was one in which the state controlled the economy and a benevolent party controlled the state and managed affairs *on behalf of* the masses. Mugabe's aim was a one-party state. When asked, 'Do you see your party joining with Mr Joshua Nkomo's ZAPU ... to form a single party instead of the present government coalition?' he replied: 'As a single party? Well, that's the ultimate goal ...'[43] Nathan Shamuyarira told me that ZANU-PF was in favour of a 'grass-root kind of democracy, debate and discussion from the bottom to the top'.[44] However, what this meant was rank-and-file participation in decision-making, within the framework of ZANU-PF's monopoly of political power. The flow of discussion would be, as he emphasised, 'from the bottom to the top'; in the light of this discussion, decisions would be taken *at the top* by the central committee. There was no room in this schema for rank-and-file *control* of the party and the state.

ZANU-PF's hostility to the post-election strikes was entirely logical, then. Workers, by raising their own demands at an inconvenient time, were disrupting the scenario laid down by the central committee. Shamuyarira said of independent trade unions that 'we want them to blossom with the full backing of the party' and even said that strikes in state concerns would be permitted.[45] But it seemed likely that Mugabe's aim was a trade-union movement, controlled by the party, which could be used as both a means to put pressure on foreign companies and of controlling rank-and-file action. Edgar Tekere's 'radicalism' is also easily understandable. This party baron, with his Jaguar and retinue of guerilla bodyguards, regarded ZANU-PF as the state — such was the logic of the liberated areas, where the peasants were organised within the framework of the party. His impatience reflected the slowness with which the unity of party and state was being realised. The incident which led to his arrest began, it was alleged, when off-duty soldiers fired on ZANLA guerillas under Tekere's command. This, Tekere seems to have believed, was an affront to the party and state. *L'etat c'est moi.*

Such a party was likely to become the instrument of the African middle classes rather than of the workers and peasants. According to one estimate there are 20,000 black businessmen in Zimbabwe, the majority of them small traders. Their advancement hitherto blocked by the settler state, their share of productive capital was negligible: the same estimate suggests that they account for 10 per cent of gross manufacturing and commercial output, 7.5 per cent of urban employment and 3 per cent of rural employment.[46] Then there was the small group of rich peasants in the TTLs and former African purchase areas, employers of 'ultra-cheap' — and ultra-exploited — family- and wage-labour.[47] Both groups would stand to gain the most from a land reform aimed at the less efficient white farmers (black businessmen often own farms). Such a reform could stimulate the formation of an indigenous bourgeoisie — a development hitherto prevented by the white monopoly of political power.[48] Finally, there was the large group of Africans with a secondary or even university education. They would stand to gain most from Africanisation; white rule meant that in 1969 37.31 per cent of the non-African working population were employed in the public sector.[49]

All these groups — African businessmen, commercial farmers and educated middle class — could enjoy significant improvements at the expense of the settlers without seriously threatening the interests of the multinationals. If, as some observers suggested, the white population fell to 100,000 by the end of 1981 there would be considerable scope for African advancement within the framework of continued foreign domination of the economy. Nor was considerable state intervention in the economy in itself a threat to foreign capital. As long ago as the second world war the government had taken over steel works and cotton mills. The state's economic role increased markedly after UDI. In 1965-77 state sources accounted for no less than 40 per cent of gross fixed capital formation.[50] ZANU-PF would no doubt use the economic power inherited from the settlers to increase the African share of productive capital. As elsewhere in the third world, the state would provide the means for the development of national capitalism, with ZANU-PF filling the vacuum left by the absence of a strong indigenous bourgeoisie.[51]

The argument would come over *how much* state control. Nathan Shamuyarira claimed that ZANU-PF's eventual goal was that of the nationalisation of all the multinational interests in mining, agriculture and manufacturing. This in itself would not be socialism but state capitalism. However, a confrontation with foreign capital was unlikely to succeed without the mobilisation of the masses and the dismantling of the state constructed to defend the existing order. Yet such a radical course might sweep away the African propertied classes along with the rest. More likely was 'the surface modification of the old society' — the substitution of the black middle classes for the settlers as western capital's junior partner in Zimbabwe. When asked for his model, Mugabe replied, 'Kenya, Tanzania, Zambia' — all three countries that have failed to break foreign capital's hold since independence.[52]

The danger to such a dependent capitalism would come from those who had supported ZANU-PF during the war. A land reform, even if it benefitted chiefly a black kulak class, would, because of the persistence of pre-capitalist kinship relations in both town and country, lead to a significant redistribution of wealth, which might dampen opposition among the peasantry. In the towns the boom stimulated by the end of sanctions and of the war might soak up some discontent, but in the long term, with population rising at a rate of 3.8 per cent a year, the frustration of the unemployed would be difficult to contain, and might merge with the militancy of workers expected to accept low wages as the price of foreign investment. Such pressures might push Mugabe leftwards in rhetoric and, perhaps, measures. Indeed, in a speech he made in early November 1980 at Mount Darwin in an area where the war had been at its bloodiest and where many peasants had been forced into protected villages, Mugabe threatened to take over white farm-land without compensation. Officials hastened to explain that his remarks applied only to unused land — many white farms in the area had been left vacant because of the war — and that there was no change in government policy.[53]

The future seemed to contain a number of unpleasant possibilities. One was a South African-backed 'destabilisation' of Zimbabwe, exploiting popular disillusionment. *The Observer* quoted a 'Pretoria informant, who has army connections' after the South African diplomatic mission in Salisbury was expelled in July 1980 to the effect that 'advisers to ... P.W. Botha are divided on Zimbabwe', with one group advocating 'economic, political and military action that would keep Zimbabwe weak and insecure, and, if possible, bring down Mugabe'.[54] Nor could a coup by the black professional army Mugabe was attempting to create be ruled out — in Algeria the liberation army which had for the most part sat out the war of independence in Tunisia intervened to topple the leftish Ben Bella government after victory.

No left alternative emerged from within ZANU-PF to challenge Mugabe. The behaviour of the ZANU and ZIPA's 'leftists' after their release from detention in Mozambique in January 1980 suggested that their radicalism was shallow. Rugare Gumbo and Mukutu Hamadziripi joined Sithole's ZANU, a rump backed by Libya and (until Amin's downfall) Uganda. Dzinashe Machingura, a maoist, joined the Moscow-backed PF. His former ally, Elias Hondo, joined the UANC. Their 'marxism-leninism' was skin-deep, a radical version of nationalism which proved in the event to be less tough-minded than that of the ZANU-PF old guard around Mugabe. Nor was Edgar Tekere a revolutionary — indeed, he had played the main role in purging ZANU-PF of this 'left wing'.

The prospects for radical change in Zimbabwe would depend on two issues. The first was the question of the black working class — would it remain submerged in the broader nationalist movement or would it begin to assert its own distinctive claims, not simply for a larger share of the national income but for political power? Potentially the African working class was the most powerful force in a society where the mass of the population were becoming progressively proletarianised, capable of welding together an alliance of workers and other social layers — the unemployed, poor peasants and so on — that could open the way to a genuine transition to socialism. Such a possibility would depend on a break with the nationalist tradition, in even its most radical forms. It had served the Zimbabwean people well in the struggle against the settlers, but its day was now done.

Equally critical would be developments in South Africa. Mugabe's politic treatment of relations with Pretoria merely crystallised a trend in the black states of the region. Mozambique, for example, had since independence remained heavily dependent on the foreign exchange earnings generated by the use made of Maputo by South African industry. In February 1979 South Africa and Mozambique signed an agreement which set rail tariffs on the Johannesburg-Maputo line at levels lower than those on the Johannesburg-Durban line in an effort to encourage the industries of the Witwatersrand to use the former route. By 1980 South Africa was supplying Mozambique with 40 per cent of her imports, compared with 19 per cent in 1974.[55] The closure of the Benguela railway as a result of the Angolan war and the teething problems of the Tanzara line connecting Lusaka and Dar-es-Salaam forced Zambia and Zaire to use South African ports for their import-export traffic. And in global economic terms Pretoria overshadowed the rest of southern Africa. In 1977 South Africa accounted for 47 per cent of the region's population, 77 per cent of its gross national product, 75 per cent of its imports, and 72 per cent of its exports.[56]

ZANU-PF's victory was followed by efforts to free the black states of the region from Pretoria's domination. In April 1980 the African leaders of southern and central Africa gathered in Lusaka to discuss ways of developing links between their economies to reduce their dependence on South Africa. Hardly had the conference ended when the South African Airways began its first scheduled flight to Lusaka (it had been due to start at the same time as the conference, but was put off to avoid embarrassing Kaunda). South African sales to Zambia doubled in the first nine months of 1979, rising from K22.5 million in the same period of 1978 to K49.4.[57] Nor did Mugabe allow worsening relations with Pretoria to affect the economic ties between the two countries, leading the *Financial Times* to comment: 'Mugabe puts maize before politics'[58] (Zimbabwe was at the time importing maize from South Africa to make up a short-fall in local production). Zimbabwe stood to gain the most from the sort of economic links discussed in Lusaka, since it was one of the most industrialised countries in the continent. A regional common market that excluded South Africa would soon be awash with cheap Zimbabwean manufactures. Ironically, given the major role played by South African companies in the Zimbabwean economy, Mugabe could end up as Pretoria's trojan horse in the rest of southern Africa.

The *Economist* reflected that 'Piet Botha's "constellation of states" policy for the region is indeed in better shape than either he or his critics appear to believe.'[59] A senior South African official told *The Times*:

> In the early months of 1980 our trade with black Africa, including countries like Nigeria, which is always roundly attacking us in public, has risen by 84 per cent. The economies of Mozambique and Zimbabwe depend so heavily on us that we are even prepared to help Maputo or Salisbury improve their direct road and rail links; this is in our interest.[60]

The economic stranglehold South Africa enjoyed over the rest of the region could be broken only through the overthrow of the apartheid regime. Mugabe's 'good neighbour' policy towards Pretoria would leave Zimbabwe and the other black states in southern and central Africa unwilling members of P.W. Botha's 'constellation'. Revolution in South Africa was a precondition of the genuine liberation of the entire region. The rest of this book will, therefore, be devoted to examining the prospects for change in the citadel of white power itself.

4. South Africa — The Roots of the Crisis

South Africa today is an extreme case of the law of uneven and combined development. Its three main characteristics may be summarised as follows. First, it is a capitalist social formation, in which the mass of the population have been separated from the means of production and therefore, in order to live, must sell their labour-power to the small minority which enjoys exclusive possession of these means of production and which is itself divided into a set of competing capitals geared to the accumulation of surplus-value extracted from the wage-labourers they employ. Second, South Africa, despite the fact that the contribution of manufacturing to its gross domestic product is greater than that of mining and agriculture combined, remains a peripheral formation in the world economy, importing the bulk of its capital goods and dependent for foreign exchange on western investment and the products of its primary industries, above all gold. Third and uniquely, the overwhelming majority of the population, including most of the industrial working class, is denied both in law and in fact, on the ground of colour, the civil and political rights to which even the most backward dictatorship elsewhere pays lip service. In this chapter we shall try to indicate briefly how these features came into being and how they underlie the crisis which shook South Africa in the course of the 1970s.

Apartheid and Capitalism

Lenin wrote that the development of capitalism could proceed along one of two roads, which he called the Prussian and the American:

> Bourgeois development may proceed by having big landlord economies at the head, which gradually become

> more and more bourgeois and gradually substitute bourgeois for feudal modes of exploitation. It may also proceed by having small peasant economies at the head, which in a revolutionary way, will remove the 'excrescence' of the feudal latifundia from the social organism and then freely develop without them along the path of capitalist economy.[1]

Capitalism in South Africa took the first, Prussian road, based upon the expropriation of the African peasantry by white settler landowners and the establishment of repressive forms of labour control in mining and agriculture. It is the continued dependence of South African capitalism on 'labour repression' that accounts for the apartheid system.

Racial oppression has been a failure of South African society since the Dutch East India Company established a settlement at the Cape to provide its ships with fresh food and water in 1652. The first two centuries of white colonisation were characterised by pre-capitalist forms of exploitation — slavery and indentured labour at the Cape and, further inland, feudal relations of production with settler farmers extracting rent in cash, kind or labour services from the African peasantry, who remained as 'squatters' on the land which had been taken from them by force.

The emergence of the modern form of racial discrimination was closely bound up with the development of capitalist relations of production, which came to predominate in South Africa only as a result of the discovery of diamonds in 1867 and gold in 1886 (although capitalist agriculture based on production for export had been established in parts of the Cape and Natal earlier in the nineteenth century). Conditions of production in the gold mines (a low average ore grade, fixed gold price and high development and overhead costs) required a plentiful supply of cheap labour. This was provided by the disintegration of African agriculture, whose extensive methods of cultivation presupposed ready access to fresh land.

The expropriation of much of the African people's land by British colonialists and Afrikaner settlers in the course of the nineteenth century undermined the communal mode of production that had prevailed among these people. African peasants, no longer able to support themselves and their dependents out of their own production, and forced by the imposition of hut and poll taxes to earn more cash, went to work in the mines. They were recruited as short-term contract labourers and paid low wages, which reflected the fact that production in the Reserves set aside for Africans took part of the burden of reproducing labour-power. The Native Land Act of 1913 allocated 13 per cent of the land to the Reserves, too little to reproduce the population, thereby sustaining the pressure on Africans to work in the farms and mines; it also prohibited them from owning land outside the Reserves, eliminating a potential source of competition with white farmers. The migrants were controlled while in the 'white' urban areas by the pass laws, which placed restrictions on their movements, and housed in all-male compounds attached to the mines. The expansion of capitalism in agriculture led to the establishment of similarly repressive forms of labour control by white farmers, with labour tenancy providing in large parts of the country a bridge between the old feudal arrangements and fully-fledged wage-labour.

The development of capitalism in both mining and agriculture therefore rested upon 'labour-repression'. Indeed, it was upon a 'marriage of maize and gold', an alliance of mining and agricultural capital, that the Union of South Africa was founded in 1910 after the defeat of the Afrikaner republics of the Transvaal and Orange Free State by Britain in the 1899-1902 war. The Union was a compromise, reflecting the common interests that underlay the conflicts between the great mining finance houses integrated into British capitalism and the predominantly Afrikaner white farmers. Blacks were denied the vote, save to a limited extent in the Cape, while the parliamentary form of the state provided a framework within which differences between sections of the white ruling class could be articulated and reconciled. This accommodation has proved remarkably durable: with the modifications necessitated by the development of manufacturing industry, it survives to this day.

Before 1948 the South African state underwent two major crises, both of which arose from within the settler camp. The first was posed by the white working class, formed initially from predominantly British skilled men imported to perform tasks, especially in the mining industry, for which Africans did not have the training. It was then swollen by the influx of 'poor whites' into towns, many of them *bywoners*, Afrikaner tenant farmers pushed off the land by the rationalisation of agriculture. An attempt by the Chamber of Mines to cut labour-costs by ending the white monopoly of skilled jobs and replacing expensive white with cheaper black labour led in 1922 to an uprising by the white miners of the Witwatersrand which was ruthlessly suppressed by the government of Jan Smuts. In the aftermath of the Rand revolt, the Pact government was formed in 1924, a coalition of the Afrikaner Nationalists and the white Labour Party, which legally entrenched the colour bar, reserving skilled jobs for whites, and encouraged the employment of 'civilised [i.e. white, predominantly Afrikaner] labour' in the state sector. These measures did not blunt the employers' offensive in the mines, where white wages were held below the levels prevailing before 1922.

The complementary interests of mining and agricultural capital were reflected in the second major crisis of the inter-war period which led to the formation of the Fusion government in 1932 when the world depression forced South Africa off the gold standard. This decision was followed in 1934 by the fusion of J.B.M. Hertzog's ruling National Party with Smuts' South Africa Party, the latter backed by English-speaking interests; it favoured both mining and agriculture and stimulated a boom which continued until after the end of the second world war.

This boom was marked by the very rapid expansion of secondary industry, stimulated, first, by a wave of import substitution caused by the introduction of tariffs and then by the war, and, second, thanks to the establishment by successive governments of state corporations — ESCOM (electricity supply), ISCOR (iron and steel), IDC (industrial development) — whose task it was to provide the infrastructure for the industrialisation of South Africa. Yet this industrialisation led to the formation of an urban black proletariat. The war years saw a wave of African labour disputes and the expansion of the black trade unions as part of a broader movement of social and political protest — squatters' campaigns and bus boycotts in Johannesburg, peasant revolts in the Reserves, and the revival of the quiescent African National Congress. The scale of the challenge to the system represented by the black working class was brought home in 1946, when the African Mine Workers

Union called a strike around demands which amounted effectively to the destruction of the migrant labour system. It was ruthlessly crushed by the employers and the state.

Repression was, of course, nothing new. The Hertzog government had mounted a brutal offensive against African trade-union and political organisation in the late 1920s and early 1930s, while Smuts had used troops and planes to crush resistance in the Reserves. But secondary industrialisation, and the urban black working class it had created, posed a new set of problems. The ruling United Party, reflecting manufacturers' worries about the scarcity of skilled labour, advocated a gradual relaxation of the pass laws and the colour bar. Such a policy would, however, conflict with the interests of both mining capital, which still depended on the migrant labour system, and the white farmers, who were losing workers to the towns — partly because wages were higher there, partly because labour-tenants reacted to attempts by their employers to cut down the land allocated to them by abandoning the countryside. It was challenged by the opposition National Party, formed in 1934 in protest against Hertzog's decision to fuse with Smuts, and committed to reversing the defeat of 1902 and establishing an Afrikaner republic independent of Britain. The Nationalists' power-base lay in the Afrikaner farmers of the Cape and the financial institutions — notably the SANLAM and SANTAM insurance companies — which they created, but increasing influence was exercised by the Afrikaner Broederbond, a secret society dominated by middle-class intellectuals from the northern provinces and especially the Transvaal. Their solution to the challenge of the black working class was the systematic extension of the migrant labour system to the whole of the African population, in other words, an intensification of labour-repression rather than its relaxation. They called this policy *apartheid* (separation).

The Nationalists won the 1948 election, thanks chiefly to their capture of 17 extra seats in the Transvaal — six in white working-class constituencies on the Witwatersrand, where the Broederbond had just taken control of the white Mine Workers Union, the rest in rural areas where white farmers were worried about the labour crisis. The Nationalists have held office ever since. Their policies proceeded along two lines. First, Afrikaner domination of the state was institutionalised, symbolically through South Africa's withdrawal from the Commonwealth and the declaration of a republic in 1961, practically by the promotion of Afrikaner economic interests. Second, successive governments set out to generalise the migrant labour system and thereby to break the African working class.

The cornerstone of apartheid is a piece of legislation inherited from Smuts, the Blacks (Urban Areas) Consolidation Act of 1945, first introduced in 1923. Under section 10 (1) of this Act no African may remain in a prescribed (i.e. urban) area for more than 72 hours unless s/he produces proof that (a) s/he has, since birth, resided continuously there; or (b) s/he has worked continuously there for one employer for a period not less than ten years or has lawfully resided continuously there for not less than 15 years; or (c) is the dependent of any African with rights under (a) or (b); or (d) has been granted permission by a local labour bureau. The Nationalists strengthened the pass laws and applied them to women for the first time; expelled black 'squatters' from white farms and 'surplus' Africans from the towns; enforced stringent geographical segregation between the races under the Group Areas Act. A network of labour bureaux was created to police the movement of Africans between country and town. Under the Black Labour Act of 1964, every African authorised to be in a prescribed (urban) area must register at his or her local labour bureau within three days of becoming unemployed, and any male African in the 'white' rural areas and homelands (as the Reserves are now called) who wishes to be placed in employment must register with a district labour bureau. To administer these laws a vast bureaucracy was created around the Department of Bantu Administration and Development (BAD), which progressively assumed total control of urban African life, notably after responsibility for the black townships was transferred from the white municipalities to 22 regional boards subordinate to BAD in 1971. There thus took shape a massive engine of repression and control designed to atomise the African working class and prevent any organised workers' movement developing.[2]

The ideological rationale of apartheid was provided by the notion of separate development, according to which there exist a number of distinct *nations* in South Africa — the whites and the various African tribes. Legislation was passed conferring powers of self-government upon the (government-appointed) tribal authorities in the Reserves, renamed Homelands but more usually known as Bantustans. Under H.F. Verwoerd, prime minister 1958-66 and the main architect of apartheid, the Nationalists adopted a policy of self-determination for the Homelands whose ultimate implication was that of granting independence to them. This policy justified the enforcement of apartheid and the denial of political rights to Africans, since they were, it could be argued, in the same position as, say, a Spanish immigrant worker in West Germany, with citizen rights in their own Bantustans, but the status only of aliens in the white areas (some 87 per cent of the country).

This policy was summed up by the Minister of Bantu Administration and Development, Blaar Coetzee, in 1972:

> (1) Every Bantu person, wherever he may find himself, is a member of his specific nation;
> (2) the Bantu in white areas, whether they are born here or whether they were allowed to come here under our control laws, are here for the labour they are being allowed to perform;
> (3) the fundamental citizenship rights may only be enjoyed by a Bantu person within his own ethnic context, attached to his own homeland;
> (4) the maximum number of people must be present in their own homelands;
> (5) the Bantu persons who are in white South Africa are treated by us as homogeneous communities;
> (6) insofar as the Bantu are secondarily present in white areas, we see to it in every possible respect that the necessary liason exists between them and their peoples in their own homelands.[3]

The Vorster adminstration (1966-78) proceeded to carry separate development into practice. The first homeland to achieve (formal) independence was the Transkei in October 1976, and it was followed by Bophuthatswana and Venda. In each case the people belonging to the tribal groups concerned were deprived of their South African citizenship. Connie Mulder declared on taking charge of BAD in February 1978: 'if our policy is taken to its logical conclusion ... there will not be one black man with South African citizenship'.[4]

The destruction of black political and trade-union organisation was both the condition of apartheid's success and its objective. It took 15 years — from 1948 to the Rivonia trial of 1963 — to crush black resistance, a process symbolised by the massacres of African demonstrators at Sharpeville and Langa in March 1960. The 1950s were a period of low and uncertain growth, a situation that in part reflected the doubts of foreign, and much local, capital about the Nationalists' strategy, but which also helped to push black workers on the defensive, just as the 1934-45 boom fuelled African militancy. Industrial capital, while critical of those aspects of apartheid which affected its interest, especially the extension of the statutory colour bar, fell in behind the government during the Sharpeville crisis. Anglo-American, despite the fact that Harry Oppenheimer was one of the Nationalists' leading white critics, came to the rescue when money poured out of South Africa after the massacre. To stem the outflow of foreign capital (R200 million in 1960 alone), one Anglo subsidiary raised a $30 million loan, Oppenheimer's American associate, Charles Engelhard, launched a company to attract US capital back into the country and Anglo helped the government arrange a loan with the Chase Manhattan Bank.[5] Once it became clear that the regime had been successful in crushing all black opposition, foreign capital poured into the country, attracted by the low wages and high profits, fuelling a prodigious boom. Between 1960 and 1970 the South African economy grew, in real terms, at an annual rate of seven per cent.[6] During that same period South Africa's foreign liabilities almost doubled, while direct foreign investment rose from R1,819 million to R3,943 million.[7]

The initial conflict of interest between the Nationalists and manufacturing capitals should not, in any case, be over-stated. The Board of Trade and Industry had argued on behalf of private capital in 1945 that 'the extension of manufacturing industry can be stimulated ... through increased mechanisation so as to derive the full benefit of the large resources of comparatively low-paid non-European labour' while white workers should be 'raised to the status of an aristocracy of labour'.[8] As we shall see, precisely this pattern was to characterise capital accumulation under Nationalist rule. Capitalism and racial oppression continued to reinforce each other in South Africa after 1948.

Contradictions

The process of capital accumulation in the 1960s and 1970s proved to be highly contradictory. Four main contradictions developed in the course of the boom, and underlay the economic and political crisis which broke out in 1973: South Africa's continued dependence on primary exports, the tendency towards growing capital intensity in all sectors, the expansion of the economic role of the state, and, most fundamentally, the growing power of black labour.

Until the 1950s South African manufacturing industry was confined largely to the production of consumer goods; thereafter, heavy industry — cars, chemicals, engineering — began to set the pace. The result was that manufacturing came to outdistance mining and agriculture, accounting for 28.1 per cent of gross domestic product in 1976 as compared with 8.1 per cent from mining and 7.3 per cent from agriculture.[9] However, the South African economy is still unable to provide all its physical constituents from its own output. In particular, it has not become self-sufficient in the production of means of production, with the result that the expansion of heavy industry had required a constant inflow of capital goods, which constitute South Africa's largest import item, averaging between 40 and 50 per cent of the country's annual import bill. Every phase of rapid growth has led to a balance of payment crisis caused by the rise in imports of plant and equipment.

Such a dependence on imported capital goods is characteristic of the middle-income 'newly industrialising countries' in the third world (Brazil, Mexico, Argentina, Taiwan, Hong Kong, Singapore), to which category South Africa properly belongs.[10] As a consequence, South Africa has a very open economy — one rand of goods and services must be imported for every four rand spent.[11] Foreign exchange must be found to purchase these imports. There have been two sources, foreign investment and export earnings, the latter making up no less than 29.6 per cent of gross domestic product in 1976.[12] However, unlike the other 'newly industrialising countries', South Africa has not been able to become a significant exporter of manufactured goods. This reflects, in part, the fact that labour productivity in manufacturing industry is very low, and is rising only very slowly (0.6 per cent a year in 1970-78).[13] A recent study showed that the most competitive South African exports are principally raw materials, while of manufactured goods those produced in the capital-intensive chemicals and metal industries are the most competitive, those produced in certain labour-intensive industries the least.[14] Among the reasons that can be given for this situation are: the inefficiencies caused by apartheid, which keeps skilled labour expensive and limits labour mobility; the restricted nature of the home market, caused in part by low African wages, which prevents firms, for example in the car industry, from exploiting economies of scale; and import controls, which have encouraged the growth of small and relatively inefficient labour-intensive firms. Furthermore, South African manufacturers' natural markets in the rest of African have been largely closed to them for political reasons: 19 per cent of South African exports went to other African countries in 1964, 18.6 per cent in 1971, and only 9.3 per cent in the first nine months of 1977.[15]

The result is that South Africa is still heavily dependent for its export earnings on the more or less processed products of mining and agriculture (see Table 7). As a consequence:

> South Africa remains a peripheral economy, in spite of its considerable growth and in spite of its substantial capacity to attract foreign investment ... Its expansion continues to be heavily import dependent, at the same time as its capacity to earn foreign exchange continues to be limited by the fact that its access to export markets is still largely confined to a restricted range of primary commodities.[16]

The South African ruling class, whatever their aspirations to autarky, remain dependent partners of western capitalism. Furthermore, the country's economic prosperity is bound up with the fluctuations of the world economy. In particular, gold remains of crucial importance to the South African economy. Gold exports are still the biggest earner of foreign exchange (see Table 8) and play a crucial role in off-setting trade deficits and financing exports.

Moreover, these crucial export industries are particularly labour-repressive. This is most obviously true in the case of the mining industry, which continues to rely on the migrant labour system to provide and discipline its workforce. The massive state investment projects designed to extend South Africa's role as a producer and processor of raw materials, and the plans to transform it into a major exporter of coal (a commodity for which the world market is rapidly growing), expanding exports from 15.4 million tonnes in 1978 to 46 million tonnes in the mid-1980s,[17] will merely reinforce the country's subordinate position within the international division of labour and her rulers' dependence on highly repressive forms of labour-control.

Table 7: South African Exports Classified by Types of Production

	Primary	Processed percentages	Manufactured
1969	38.7	37.5	23.8
1970	36.0	38.6	25.4
1971	36.9	37.1	26.0
1972	38.5	38.6	22.9
1973	36.0	39.0	25.0
1974	35.4	43.1	21.5
1975	39.5	39.7	20.8

Source: Nedbank Group Economic Unit, *South Africa: an economic appraisal*, Johannesburg, 1977, p.5.

Table 8: Net gold output as a percentage of South Africa's total foreign receipts

1960	1965	1970	1971	1972	1973	1974	1975	1976
32.3	35.9	29.2	29.3	28.1	33.7	37.7	33.6	27.3

Source: *South Africa: an economic appraisal* p.206.

The second major feature of capitalist development in South Africa is that it has involved considerable mechanisation. The figures available (see Table 9) suggest that what Marx called the organic composition of capital, the ratio between capital invested in plant and equipment and capital advanced to purchase labour-power, has risen sharply in South Africa as a result of the trend towards mechanisation. This development has not been confined to manufacturing industry. In mining the capital employed per worker rose in real terms at an annual 3.2 per cent in 1946-70 and then jumped very sharply in 1973-76, when the real fixed capital stock rose by 28 per cent while employment fell by two per cent.[18] Similar trends have been displayed in agriculture (see Table 10) where government tax policies encourage mechanisation and the centralisation and concentration of capital, leading to a fall in labour costs as a total proportion of farming costs from 68 per cent in 1948 to 29 per cent in 1973.[19]

Table 9: Capital-Labour Ratios in South Africa, 1946-77

	Real fixed capital stock per economically active person (R at constant 1970 prices)			Annual rate of increase percentage	
	1946	1970	1977	1946-70	1970-77
All sectors	1726	3294	4146	2.7	3.3
Manufacturing	1216	2689	3818	3.4	5.4

Source: C.J. Swanepoel and J. Van Dyk, 'The fixed capital stock and sectoral capital-output ratios of South Africa, 1946 to 1947', *South African Reserve Bank Quarterly Bulletin*, September 1978, pp.36, 38.

Table 10: South African Agricultural Production, 1946-75

Year	*Production Units*	*Tractors*	*Value of Production (Rm)*	*Volume of Production (1960=100)*
1946	112,453	20,292	252.5	53
1950	116,848	48,422	447.2	68
1955	111,586	87,451	698.5	84
1960	105,859	119,196	814.6	100
1965	95,438	138,422	1,039.9	119
1970	90,422	157,127	1,516.2	159
1975	77,591	167,981	2,729.0	170

Source: *South African Statistics, 1978*, Pretoria: Government Printers, 1978, 9.4.

One consequence is very high levels of African unemployment. A business economist estimated that there were two million black unemployed in May 1978, 20 per cent of the economically active population.[20] The character of capital accumulation in South Africa bears a number of similarities to the pattern of development in the 'newly industrialising countries', where the rapid expansion of manufacturing industry has been secured thanks to considerable state intervention, wholesale repression and large-scale foreign investment. But, as Nigel Harris explains, rapid capital accumulation in these countries does not prevent very high levels of unemployment:

> Today levels of labour-productivity, determined in technically advanced capitalism, ensure that industrial output can be expanded very rapidly without proportionately increasing the employment of labour ... Instead of the industrial economy expanding to encompass the potential labour force of a whole country, it tends to remain limited to a small enclave of high growth with relatively few effects on the mass of the rural population.[21]

The migrant labour system is one method of sustaining this pattern of capital accumulation. The Bantustans are in no sense self-sufficient economic units. The Transkei government itself acknowledged that 'one can hardly speak of a Transkei economy in any meaningful sense; more properly one must call it a labour reserve'. The 'state' is forced to import some two-thirds of its food requirements and to export more than 60 per cent of its male labour-force as migrant contract workers in the 'white' areas.[22] One study suggests that some 60 per cent of all rural households in the Transkei depend for their reproduction on the sale of labour-power, leading to a situation in which the men go to work in the 'white' areas while women are responsible for the bulk of wage-labour and subsistence agricultural production in the Transkei.[23]

The Transkei pattern was reproduced in other Bantustans. In 1980 Kwazulu was struck by one of the worst droughts in Zulu history. Cases of child malnutrition increased sharply; it was feared that as many as 500,000 cattle, one quarter of the Zulu herd which is the homeland's main source of internally generated wealth, might die. Nicholas Ashford wrote in *The Times*:

> The drive from the Indian Ocean coast through the

> European-owned sugar plantations up into the hills of Zululand provides dramatic evidence not just of the effect of the drought but of how the government's homeland policy is steadily debilitating the land and people of Kwazulu.
>
> Although European farmers have also been affected by the drought they have on the whole been able to compensate for the lack of rainfall by irrigation. The relative greenness of their sugarcane plantations contrasts starkly with the dry, burnt-out fields of the Zulus.

A church worker at Tugela Ferry, where only four per cent of the topsoil was left, attributed this to overcrowding caused by resettlement of blacks from white areas, which had trebled the local population.[24]

Disaster areas though they are, the Bantustans are essential to the reproduction of capitalism in South Africa. They act as a 'labour-reserve', providing a pool of cheap black labour-power for the white-owned factories, mines and farms, and at the same time serve as dumping grounds for 'surplus' workers and the 'superfluous appendages' of the workforce in white areas — the unemployed and the unemployable. In other words, the Bantustans provide the institutional framework through which the industrial reserve army generated by South Africa's highly capital-intensive pattern of growth is organised and controlled.[25]

The policy of resettlement fitted into this pattern. A government circular in 1967 declared that 'no stone is to be left unturned to achieve the settlement in the homelands of non-productive Bantu at present residing in the European areas'. The 'non-productive' included 'the aged, the unfit, widows with dependent children', 'Bantu on European farms who become superfluous as a result of age [or] disability', 'Bantu squatters', and 'professional Bantu'. By 1975 some three million Africans had either been resettled or scheduled for resettlement in the Bantustans. In 1978 the government took wider powers to deport 'idle or undesirable' blacks from the urban areas. Pass law arrests in the cities rose from 173,571 in 1977 to 272,887 the following year:

> Exporting the unemployed to the Bantustans is a logical extension of the doctrine that the presence of Africans in

> the 'white' areas is to be tolerated only for so long as they are required to 'minister' to white needs. Indeed, influx control already serves as a means of confining unemployed Africans to the Bantustans in the sense that African living there are not allowed to enter the 'white' areas to look for work but must instead remain in the Bantustans in the hope that they will be requisitioned and recruited under the migratory labour system.[26]

The South African state has not only assumed responsibility for organising and regulating the supply of labour-power. It has increasingly become productive capitalist in its own right. State corporations dominate a number of sectors — ISCOR (iron and steel), ESCOM (electricity), Sasol (coal and oil), Natref (oil refining), Alusaf (aluminium), in addition to the Industrial Development Corporation (IDC), which has interests in a number of sectors. The share of the state in productive capital has been growing rapidly, notably in manufacturing, where in 1970-77 the real fixed capital stock of public corporations rose by nearly 17 per cent a year (compared to an annual rate of 9 per cent in the 1960s), while in the private sector the rate of growth of real fixed capital stock halved, from 9 per cent a year in the 1960s to 4.5 per cent a year in 1970-77.[27] The rising gold price in the early 1970s encouraged Vorster and his finance minister, Nico Diedrichs, to undertake an ambitious programme of state-controlled investment projects, notably a series of coal-fired power stations (R5.8 billion), an increase in steel-producing capacity to 6.5 million tons a year (R2.67 million), the deep sea harbour at Richards Bay (for the Natal coal mines) and the 861 kilometres Sishen-Saldhana railway to transport exports of iron ore (together R3 billion), the Sasol II coal-into-oil project (R2.5 billion) and the nuclear power station at Koeburg in the Cape (R970 million).

These investments were financed by heavy foreign borrowing by the state and contributed to a sharp rise in the public sector's share of the economy (see Table 11). Government expenditure doubled in the three years to 1976, leading to a huge increase in the money supply (which rose at an annual rate of 20 per cent in 1972-76),[28] and double-digit inflation. The characteristic pattern of the business cycle in South Africa — rapid expansion, a sharp rise in imports, followed by a balance of payments crisis — combined with the government's inflationary policies and the abrupt fall in the gold price in 1974-75 precipitated in 1976 what the *Financial Mail* called 'the longest and deepest recession in the South African economy for at least 45 years'.[29] The Vorster-Diedrichs boom and its aftermath crystallised the fears of both Afrikaner and English-speaking businessmen that they would be suffocated by the ever-expanding state sector. Andreas Wassenaar, head of the Afrikaner business empire centred around SANLAM, and a member of the Broederbond, scandalised the Nationalist establishment by publishing a book denouncing the trend towards state capitalism. He wrote:

> Economic history in the Republic of South Africa has produced an officialdom — including a bureaucracy which is extremely Afrikaner-orientated — which is extremely lukewarm if not antagonistic in its attitude towards private enterprise and certainly vehemently opposed to the profit motive to a degree which, in the long run, threatens the future of capitalism.[30]

Table 11: Total Public Spending as a Percentage of Gross Domestic Expenditure, 1960-76

1960	1965	1970	1971	1972	1973	1974	1975	1976
17.2	22.3	23.7	25.9	27.9	24.7	26.1	30.1	31.8

Source: *South Africa: an economic appraisal*, p.249.

The Black Working Class

Most serious of all for the apartheid economy was its continued dependence on black labour (see Table 12). The expansion of manufacturing industry (whose output rose at an annual rate of 5.7 per cent in 1961-77)[31] continued to suck blacks into the urban areas, while the attempt to transform the African working class into migrant labourers failed. In 1970 there were four million African workers in the 'white' areas, of which only 1.3 million were male migrants; settled black workers amounted to 1.1 million in the urban areas, 1.6 million in the rural areas. In 1970-77 the African labour force rose by 1.6 million (30.4 per cent), while the white labour force rose by 300,000 (21.7 per cent); the increase caused the proportion of whites in the total labour force to fall from 19.6 per cent to 18.7 per cent in the same period, while Africans' share rose from 68.8 per cent to 70.5 per cent.[32]

Table 12: South Africa's Economically Active Population, 1976.

	number (thousands)	percentage
Whites	1,802	17.9
Coloureds	809	8.0
Asians	229	2.3
African	7,216	71.8
Total	10,056	100.0

Source: *South African Statistics, 1978*, 7.5.

The process of capital accumulation in the 1960s and 1970s did not merely lead to an increase in the numbers of black workers. It also involved a transformation of the labour process, closely connected to the rising capital-intensity of production — 'deskilling', i.e. the reduction in the skill content of work performed and the destruction of craft control over the process of production, together with an expansion in the numbers of the so-called 'new middle class' — white-collar, professional and supervisory workers — and of the semi-skilled workers performing such tasks as machine-minding.[33] In South Africa whites have tended to move out of manual jobs into the 'new middle class', while Africans make up the bulk of semi-skilled as well as unskilled workers.[34] Behind the apartheid legislation reserving skilled jobs for whites, a process known as 'fragmentation' or 'dilution' took place, involving shifting the colour-bar upwards as skilled jobs formerly held by whites were broken up into a number of simpler tasks performed by less skilled — and cheaper — blacks. The Wiehahn commission (see chapter 5 below) acknowledged that:

> a process of restructuring of work categories to utilise available skills better and to create semi-skilled tasks for relatively unskilled workers — mainly blacks ... has become a permanent feature of the process of industrialisation in the country's main centres.[35]

This process was stimulated also by an endemic shortage of skilled and white-collar labour. Only 16.5 per cent of the economically active population in South Africa were employed in professional and technical, administrative and executive and clerical and sales jobs in 1970 compared to a norm of 18 to 20 per cent in other newly industrialising countries. This reflected a shortage of the white workers who monopolised these categories. On one estimate, if a 5 per cent growth rate were assumed, there would be 2,796,000 white employees in demand in 1990, but only 1,348,000 whites available. During the boom years of the 1960s and early 1970s this shortage was offset by the ready availability of foreign capital and by 'dilution', but as the crisis of the mid-1970s unfolded, it became clear that more radical solutions were necessary.[36]

Ironically, then, the boom unleashed by the Nationalists' defeat of the black resistance led to the economy's *increased* dependence on African labour. The implications of this change were brought home to white South Africa in 1973 when a wave of spontaneous mass strikes involving some 100,000 black workers shook the Durban-Pinetown area. Even the official statistics (see Table 13) reveal a huge leap in black industrial militancy. The response of the employers and the state to the strikers was quite mild: only 207 strikers, 0.2 per cent of the total, were prosecuted compared to 822 — 24 per cent of all those striking — in 1959,[37] and legislation was introduced conceding Africans the right to strike.

One study of the strikes offers these reasons for the comparative moderation of both government and bosses:

> One of the employers' representatives to whom we spoke explained the absence of massive arrests, and the fact that those firms who dismissed their staff re-engaged most of them, by saying that 'it is too jolly difficult to get a labour force as it is'. He pointed out that groups of unskilled workers can be sent back to the homelands, but this is impossible when there are strikes all over. Moveover, when workers are a bit more skilled employers no longer want a high labour turnover ... The proportion of African workers in the workforce is increasing. The total number of African workers in the urban workforce is increasing. The number of African workers doing jobs that require some sort of training is increasing. The traditional artisan plus

several unskilled labouring assistants is being replaced by the machine-minding operative who requires several weeks' training and several months' production in order to reach the normal level of production. All these factors mean that the potential bargaining power of African workers is increasing.[38]

Table 13: Industrial Disputes Involving Blacks in South Africa 1965-78

	No. of persons involved	Strike days
1965	3,540	2,492
1966	3,253	3,297
1968*	1,705	1,361
1969	4,232	3,980
1970	3,303	3,050
1971	4,196	3,316
1972	8,814	13,774
1973	98,029	229,137
1974	58,975	98,396
1975	23,295	18,720
1976	26,931	22,325
1977	15,091	15,099
1978	14,095	10,536

* No figures given for 1967

Source: *South African Statistics, 1978*, 7.23.
Survey of Race Relations in South Africa, 1979, p.286.

The mid-1970s saw this bargaining power reflected at a number of levels. African trade unions, although they enjoyed only a twilight semi-legal existence, rarely recognised by the employers, never by the state, grew rapidly in this period. The Wiehahn commission estimated that at the end of 1977 there were 27 black trade unions organising between 55,000 and 70,000 workers.[39] Their growth and the strike wave itself were stimulated by the rapid rise in prices, itself a result of the Vorster-Diedrichs boom. Employers were quite ready to concede wage-increases — a shift in attitude reflecting the capital-intensity of industrial production, which meant that labour-costs had fallen as a proportion of total costs — as well as the economic muscle their greater skill gave black workers. In 1970-75 African wages rose in real terms at an annual 6.6 per rate cent, while white wages rose by only one per cent. The black-white wage gap fell for the first time in 1973-75, from R2,815 to R2,724 (in constant 1970 prices), while the black share in personal income rose by 6 per cent in 1970-75, from 26 to 32 per cent. These increases were unevenly distributed (the figures for wage rises exclude agricultural and domestic workers), affected migrant labourers far less than urban workers, and still left the white/black income ratio at 11:1 in 1975. However, as one economist pointed out, 'this is the first time in South Africa's economic history that such a redistribution has taken place'.[40]

The mines, still as we have seen central to South African capitalism's prosperity, were also shaken by black labour unrest which resulted in 178 dead and 1,043 injured in 1972-76.[41] Despite this brutal response, the Chamber of Mines, like other employers, was prepared to pay more: black miners' wages rose fivefold in 1970-75, increasing from 14 per cent of working costs in 1970 to 25 per cent in 1975.[42] This policy reflected in part the Chamber's worries about labour supplies, especially after the Malawian government banned recruitment of its citizens for the South African mines and Frelimo took over in Mozambique. The mining houses responded by stepping up recruitment among the unemployed and underemployed of the homelands, especially the Transkei and Kwazulu, and of the rural 'white' areas, of the Cape and Natal in particular. South Africans rose from 20 per cent to 44 per cent of the black workforce in the mines between 1973 and 1975.[43]

This shift in the balance of power between white capital and black labour underlay the Soweto uprising, even if it was the victories of Mozambique and Angola that provided the inspiration, and the tyranny and inhumanity of 'Bantu education' the occasion, of the school-students' revolt. A number of very thorough studies of the uprising have now been published,[44] but its principal significance lay in the fact that, as John Rogers and I pointed out at the time, unlike Sharpeville — 'simply the most prominent in a series of events in which a mass movement that had fought throughout the 1950s was crushed' — 'Soweto ... is the highest point reached so far in a *rising* wave of struggles' both within the country and elsewhere in the region. 'South Africa', we wrote, 'is clearly entering a period of massive confrontation between the regime and the oppressed black population.'[45]

And so it proved to be the case. The black youth revolt which began in Soweto on 16 June 1976 spread both geographically — to the rest of the Rand and then to the Cape — and socially — from the schools to the factories. No less than three stay-at-homes — political general strikes — occurred in 1976, two in the Transvaal, on 4-6 August (100,000 on strike) and 23-25 August (132,000), and then in both the Transvaal and the Western Cape, where half-a-million African and Coloured workers downed tools on 13-16 September.[46] But the core of the revolt was the black youth of the townships, who sustained their movement throughout 1977, winning a signal victory in June, when they forced the stooge Soweto Urban Bantu Council to resign.

The eventual collapse of the revolt arose in part from the nature of its leadership — drawn largely from high-school students, a small and comparatively privileged minority of their age-group. The students only gradually groped towards a strategy connecting their demands to the conditions and grievances of black workers. The resulting failure to weld a lasting alliance between workers and students was to some degree related to the grim economic climate — wage-rises, under the impact of the recession, began to slow down late in 1976,[47] while one in ten factory workers were laid off in 1976-77.[48] Its effect was to confine the revolt to the townships, which were comparatively easy for the regime's forces to isolate and surround. Moreover, the students' main weapon — the school boycott — deprived them of the most obvious means of bringing their supporters together, within the classrooms.[49] These factors combined with sheer exhaustion, the effects of wholesale repression — 700 publicly recorded deaths, between June 1976 and October 1977, mass detentions and the suppression of the black consciousness movement on 19 October 1977 — and an exodus of thousands of young blacks into exile caused the revolt to wind down in early 1978. As we shall see, this proved to be only a temporary respite for the regime.

5. Rationalising Apartheid — Piet Botha's 'Total Strategy'

The crisis in South Africa is what Antonio Gramsci called an 'organic crisis':

> A crisis occurs, sometimes lasting for decades. This exceptional duration means that incurable structural contradictions have revealed themselves (reached maturity), and that despite this, the political forces that are struggling to conserve and defend the existing structure itself are making every effort to cure them, within certain limits, and to overcome them.[1]

We saw in the last chapter what these 'incurable structural contradictions' were in South Africa's case — her peripheral status within the world economy, the rising organic composition of capital in South African industry, the growing role of the state, and the revolt of the black working class. Since his accession to the premiership in September 1978, Piet Botha has sought to 'cure' and 'overcome' these contradictions, 'within certain limits' — those set by the continued reproduction of capitalism in South Africa. In this chapter we shall consider his ambitious 'total strategy'.

Muldergate and the Rise of P.W. Botha

To understand this strategy, we must first take account of the peculiar form of state that exists in South Africa. It is not a fascist state, but rather 'a racially exclusive bourgeois democracy', as one South African marxist put it,[2] involving a parliamentary system of government in which blacks are denied the vote. This situation reflects both the economy's continued reliance on 'labour repression' and influx control and the need for some framework within which the conflicting interests of particular fractions of capital can be expressed and to some degree reconciled. Also represented in the state, and forming the popular base of the ruling National Party, is the white working class. The loyalty of white wage-earners to the status quo was secured through a combination of economic concessions ('civilised labour', job reservation etc.), the incorporation of white trade unions in the state and the dense network of cultural and other associations built up under the aegis of Afrikaner nationalism.

The National Party, indeed, in its relation to the white working class offered an almost text-book illustration of Gramsci's notion of a hegemonic party ruling by consent as well as by force. Its ideological domination of the white masses was organised through the Federasie van Afrikaanse Kulturverenigings (FAK), a front for the Broederbond, with over 2,000 affiliated cultural, religious and youth bodies, including the three main Afrikaner churches, the Voortrekkers (scouts), and cultural associations of nurses, the defence forces and white employees in the railways and post office. The FAK organised the *Volksfeeste*, like Republic Day (31 May) and the Day of the Covenant (16 December), at which the continuity of the Afrikaner struggle for national independence was reaffirmed. Afrikanerdom also had a powerful 'organic intelligentsia', charged with articulating and developing Nationalist ideology, based in the universities, churches and press. The crux of this ideology was the notion of national self-determination, which served to justify both the Afrikaner struggle for ethnic, political and economic identity, *and* the denial of rights of Africans, since they had their own national homes in the Bantustans.[4]

Within this framework the nature of Afrikaner Nationalism has changed since the National Party came to power. In 1948 it was an alliance of the mainly rural bourgeoisie of the Cape with the northern petty bourgeoisie against the domination of 'English-speaking' capital. Nationalist governments set out to build up Afrikaner capital, both by giving government accounts and contracts to Afrikaner firms and through the expanding role of the state corporations, all controlled by Afrikaners. State backing, combined with an economic environment favourable to growth, and plentiful cheap labour, caused the Afrikaner share of the private sector (excluding agriculture) to rise from 9.6 per cent in 1948-49 to 20.8 per cent in 1975.[5] The result was the rise of Afrikaner firms such as Federale Volksbeleggings (investments), General Mining (now the third largest mining finance house), Rembrandt (tobacco and drinks), Volkskas and Nedbank (banking), SANLAM (insurance). A powerful Afrikaner financial and industrial bourgeoisie has come into being. A feature of this development has been that, as the *Financial Times* put it:

> the Afrikaner businessman now probably has as much, if not more, in common with his English-speaking counterpart in commerce, industry and mining as with the blue-collar workers, farmers, teachers and civil servants who have traditionally formed the power base of the National Party.[6]

This shared business interest was expressed after the Soweto uprising when both the Transvaal Chamber of Industries and the Afrikaanse Handelsinstitut (Afrikaans Chamber of Commerce) called on the government to accept the permanent presence of blacks in urban areas, while retaining influx control.[7]

The emergence of the Afrikaner bourgeoisie also led to changes within the Nationalist establishment, a process typified by the transformation of the Broederbond. This secret society began life as the class organisation of the northern Afrikaner petty bourgeoisie, founded in 1918 by 14 railway clerks, clergymen and policemen, and played a crucial role in the subjection of certain key white unions, notably the mineworkers, to Nationalist domination.[8] Under Verwoerd the Broeders, and their chairman, Piet Meyer, also head of the South African Broadcasting Corporation, enjoyed great influence, and came to occupy centre-stage in the mythologies of liberal critics of the regime. Pride came before a fall. Vorster effectively transformed the Broederbond into 'a mere tool of the National Party',[9] forcing Meyer to expel the supporters of his old associate, Albert Hertzog, who in 1969 broke with the government to form the far-right Herstigte Nasionale Partie (HNP). Hertzog and Meyer had directed the Nationalist takeover of the white unions, and were critical of measures such as the 1963 deal between the Afrikaner mining house Federale Mynbou and Anglo-American which allowed the former to take over

General Mining. Vorster resisted Broederbond-instigated moves to have the state break up Anglo-American as a step towards imposing Afrikaner economic domination.[10] The subordination of the Broederbond to the government was shown in 1974 when Professor Gerrit Viljoen, a prominent *verlig* (enlightened) intellectual, ousted Andries Treurnicht, the Broederbond's ultra-*verkramp* (reactionary) chairman.

The clash between Vorster and Hertzog was also a conflict between the Cape and the Transvaal. The National Party is a federal organisation, each province (Cape, Transvaal, Orange Free State and Natal) possessing its own congress, head committee and leader, while the parliamentary caucus of Nationalist MPs elects the party's national leader. When D.F.Malan formed the modern National Party in 1934 in protest against J.B.M. Hertzog's decision to fuse with Smuts, it was in the Cape alone that he had an organisation, significant parliamentary representation (14 MPs, compared to four in the OFS and one in the Transvaal) and a newspaper, *Die Burger*. However, after 1948 the Transvaal party, representing the most populous and economically important province, claimed the dominant say in Nationalist counsels, with the Broederbond acting as a formidable pressure group for their interests. When Malan retired from the premiership in 1954 he was replaced by J.G. Strijdom, 'the Lion of the North', for many years the only Nationalist MP in the Transvaal, who had the backing of Verwoerd and Albert Hertzog, rather than by the Cape leader, T.E. Dönges. Again, in 1958 it was the Transvaal candidate, Verwoerd, who became prime minister after Strijdom's death.

Thereafter, the Cape Nationalists sought to challenge northern dominance within the party. Their chief instrument was *Die Burger*, which campaigned successfully for the establishment of a parliamentary republic rather than one involving an executive presidency like the old Boer republics, the form favoured by the Broederbond. In 1965 Nasionale Pers, the Cape-based owners of *Die Burger*, established *Die Beeld*, a Johannesburg Sunday paper, against Verwoerd's wishes, in order 'to propagate Cape Nationalism in the Transvaal and undermine the ever-growing dominance of Transvaal Nationalists in the Government'. It was *Die Beeld* which opened the attack on Hertzog and the Nationalist far right in August 1966, closely followed by the rest of Nasionale Pers. Elaine

Potter in her study of the South African press, writes: 'There can be little doubt that the Afrikaans press brought about or, arguably, speeded up the first split in the National Party for 20 years.' *Die Beeld* and *Die Burger* even attacked Ben Schoeman, the leader of the Transvaal Nationalists, in 1967, with the backing of P.W. Botha. To quote Elaine Potter again: 'Nasionale Pers was trying to influence the selection of a future leader of the party, who in their terms was quite logically the leader of the Cape National Party — P.W. Botha'.[11]

This division between Cape and Transvaal within the National Party arose to some degree from differences in the Party's power base in the two provinces. The wealthy Afrikaner farmers of the Cape had created the great SANLAM financial empire, backed Malan against J.B.M. Hertzog, donated the funds for the Nationalist drive in the trade unions and provided much of the impetus behind the movement in the 1930s and 1940s to divert the savings of the *volk* into Afrikaner business interests. The Afrikaner middle class in the Transvaal were confronted with an English-speaking business establishment and a white population that was rapidly being urbanised and proletarianised. Hence the greater importance in the north of the drive for ideological hegemony, to defend the Afrikaner working class from 'alien' and subversive influences and provide a base for attaining state power. Hence also the importance — after 1948 — of the state apparatus for the Afrikaner establishment in the Transvaal, centred on Pretoria, the seat of administration.

> Whereas in the north the bureaucratic strata predominate in Afrikaner life, the salient feature in the south is the more established Afrikaner bourgeoisie of the Cape, based, more characteristically, on private wealth or professional qualifications.[12]

It was indeed the hypertrophy of the Nationalist-controlled state bureaucracy, denounced by Andreas Wassenaar on behalf of the Cape business establishment, that lay behind the Muldergate scandal. This affair centred on the use of R64 million of state funds by Eschel Rhoodie, the secretary for information, chiefly to finance an English-speaking pro-Nationalist daily paper, *The Citizen*. Despite desperate efforts by the government to limit the damage caused by revelations of

Rhoodie's activities, a number of leading Nationalist figures were implicated. Most important among them were Connie Mulder, leader of the Transvaal Nationalists and Minister of Information, General Hendrik Van Den Bergh, the widely feared chief of BOSS reputed to be Vorster's *eminence grise*, and, finally, John Vorster himself. The scandal compelled Vorster to announce in September 1978 his resignation to stand for the ceremonial post of state president. In normal circumstances Mulder could have expected to defeat the other main candidate, P.W. Botha, since the Transvaal had 80 votes in the Nationalist caucus, compared to the Cape's 55, Natal's 13 and the Orange Free State's 24. However, Pik Botha, the immensely popular *verligte* foreign minister, ran and split the Transvaal vote, preventing any candidate winning on the first ballot, when P.W. Botha got 78 votes, Mulder 72 and Pik Botha 22. In the run-off, with Pik eliminated, Botha won 98 votes, Mulder 74. For the first time in nearly 25 years the Cape had won the party leadership. Botha's control of the government was strengthened when subsequent revelations forced Mulder to resign from the government and parliament and to give up the Transvaal leadership. Finally Vorster himself was thrown to the wolves, resigning from the state presidency in June 1979 after the Erasmus commission appointed to investigate the scandal confirmed that he too had been aware of Eschel Rhoodie's activities.[13]

Muldergate, culminating as it did in the disgrace of three of the most powerful figures in the Nationalist establishment, including 'Honest John' Vorster himself, had a traumatic effect on Afrikanerdom, in whose ideology Calvinistic rectitude plays a significant part. The affair somehow summarised the changes that had occurred in Afrikanerdom. For a start it symbolised the squandering of state money to the detriment of national capital. When Wassenaar, before the scandal broke, wrote that 'the national crisis which the RSA faces is a direct consequence of overspending by the state',[14] he could have been describing the actions of the free-spending Rhoodie. Then there was the sheer corruption of the business, it was claimed that Rhoodie and his two brothers, Nico, a prominent intellectual apologist for apartheid, and Denys, deputy secretary for information, had misappropriated state funds for their own benefit, running up huge bills on expenses. And there seemed to be more dirt beneath the surface — Robert Smit, former South African representative to the IMF, and his wife were murdered in November 1977 because, it was alleged, he had uncovered the illegal transfer of funds abroad by prominent Nationalists. Finally, it brought home that the Afrikaners were no longer a rural people but part of an urban, industrialised, class-divided society. As the *Financial Mail* put it, 'the Nats are no longer the party of the *volk*. They are the better-dressed, affluent members of the *volk*'.[15] The malaise of the Afrikaner people after 30 years of Nationalist rule was diagnosed with irony and precision by Andre Brink, in novels such as *Rumours of Rain*, a study of the moral nullity of one of the new generation of Afrikaner businessmen.

The 'Brazilian model'

Piet Botha was nobody's idea of a liberal. His political career began in 1936, when he was appointed a full-time organiser of the Cape Nationalists. Although a protege of Malan's, as a back-bench parliamentarian in the 1950s he supported the hardliner Hendrik Verwoerd first for the post of minister of native affairs (as BAD was then known), then for prime minister. He became leader of the Cape party in 1966. But before coming to the premiership Botha was known chiefly for his role as Vorster's minister of defence. When he took on this portfolio in 1966 the South African Defence Force (SADF) occupied a relatively lowly position in the state apparatus, since the principal coercive role, that of suppressing internal black opposition, was performed by the South African Police (SAP). The outbreak in 1967 of liberation wars on South Africa's borders in Zimbabwe and Namibia, and the changed situation brought about in the region by the Portuguese coup, led to a reversal of positions, with the SADF assuming an increasingly important role both inside and outside the country. Botha's years as minister of defence (1966-80) saw a prodigious expansion of the armed forces and of South Africa's military-industrial complex. The defence budget rose from R36 million in 1958-59 to nearly R2 billion in 1979-80, while the turnover of the state Armaments Development and Production Corporation (Armscor) increased in 1968-78 from R32 million to R979 million. By the end of that period 800 private companies employing 100,000 workers were involved in Armscor contracts, helping South Africa to become largely self-sufficient in arms production. Thanks to the introduction of compulsory military service for white males between 18 and 45 (two years' initial service, three-month call-ups thereafter), the standing operational force rose from 11,500 in 1960 to 180,000 in 1979, and total SADF manpower from 78,000 to 494,000.[16]

Muldergate involved a struggle for power between two different branches of the repressive state apparatus. Vorster as minister of justice and police had, with the help of Van Den Bergh, then head of the security branch, crushed the black resistance in the early 1960s. After Vorster's rise to the premiership, BOSS was created with Van Den Bergh acting as his closest political adviser, for example, representing him in negotiations with Kaunda and other black leaders during detente. Van Den Bergh, however, antagonised P.W. Botha by opposing the SADF invasion of Angola in October 1975. On becoming prime minister Botha wasted no time in clipping BOSS's wings, renaming it first the Department of National Security and then the National Intelligence Service, and placing it under his control along with its rival, the Department of Military Intelligence.

Now it was the turn of the SADF, with its chief, General Magnus Malan assuming a position similar to that of Van Den Bergh under Vorster. The rise of the military was reflected in the enhanced role of the State Security Council, a committee of senior ministers, civil servants and generals, which under Botha (who initially retained the defence portfolio) became a sort of super-cabinet, meeting on Mondays, the day before the cabinet's weekly meeting, and effectively pre-empting the latter's decisions. In September 1979 Botha reduced the number of cabinet committees from 40 to five, — internal affairs, social affairs, economic affairs, foreign affairs and state security. The five committee chairmen — Piet Koornhof, Fanie Botha, Owen Horwood, Pik Botha and Alwyn Schlebusch, respectively ministers of co-operation and development, manpower utilisation, finance, foreign affairs, and interior and justice — formed with Botha an inner cabinet, by-passing both the bureaucracy (there were plans afoot to reduce the number of departments from 39 to 18) and the Nationalist party machine, especially the disgruntled Transvalers.

This centralisation of power and militarisation of the state apparatus was justified by the claim that South Africa was fighting a 'total war' which required a 'total strategy'. Botha had as minister of defence presided over the emergence of a new generation of senior officers, who made the study of counter-insurgency operations in other parts of the world — Malaya, Indochina, Algeria (where Malan actually served), Latin America — one of their main pre-occupations. They were especially interested in the case of Brazil, where after the 1964 coup the army had created a 'national security state' committed to the promotion of growth and the suppression of disorder and based on two premises:

> The first stressed the fact that national security and economic development were inter-dependent, and that since the fighting of a modern war required the active consent of the whole nation, means must be found of mobilising its will, its unity and its productive capacity. Thus in addition to its traditional requirements, national security implied planning of the national life so as to optimise production and the economy while minimising internal tensions ... According to the second concept, part of the economic backwardness found in under-developed countries was due to internal pressures resulting from the world-wide ideological struggle [between capitalism and communism] and these pressures represented a serious threat to national security.[17]

The second element, the 'total assault' against South Africa was defined by Magnus Malan in a 1977 speech as involving 'diplomacy, industry, trade, technology, the written and spoken word, the public media, demonstrations, strikes, boycotts, subversion and so on'. The enemy, then, was perceived as being, not only black nationalism and the Soviet Union, but also western capital, which showed itself ready to back an arms boycott against South Africa in November 1977. Professor Jan Lombard, an Afrikaner economist close to Botha, summed up the Nationalists' fears: 'if the present regime should become the target of liquidation by the western powers themselves, in the hope that they could replace it by a more acceptable anti-communist regime, the nature of the security problem becomes something of a nightmare'.[18] Certainly Botha adopted a less co-operative stance towards the west. What the *Economist* called 'the biggest diplomatic operation ever to be mounted in southern Africa',[19] the visit by the foreign ministers of the US, West Germany, France, Britain and Canada to Pretoria in October 1978, ended in failure when Botha and Malan refused to accept the 'contact powers' proposal for a Namibian settlement involving SWAPO and instead held 'internal' elections in December, which led to the installation of the stooge Democratic Turnhalle Alliance. Pretoria also backed the internal settlement in Zimbabwe and only reluctantly acceded to the Lancaster House agreement. In April 1979 three US military attachés were expelled from South Africa after being caught looking for secret nuclear installations (Pretoria and Washington had already had a major row in 1977 over the former's reputed possession of atomic weapons).

The rift between South Africa and the west should not, however, be exaggerated. As we saw in chapter one, the Carter administration after 1977-78 began to regard Pretoria more favourably, as a bulwark against the Russians and Cubans, while Ronald Reagan's victory in the US presidential elections would tip the balance further in Botha's favour. Similarly, despite the regime's attempts to make the economy more self-sufficent — in November 1977 the National Supplies Procurement Act was activated, empowering the government to assume direct control of the economy in the event of sanctions being imposed — South African capitalism remained heavily dependent on western imports of capital goods and on foreign investment to help finance them. Western assistance for the apartheid regime continued to be forthcoming. It was suggested, for example, that the CIA, State Department and Pentagon were involved in the supply of long-range 155mm howitzer shells to South Africa by an American firm, Space Research.[20]

Nevertheless, the notion of a total assault against South Africa served to justify the enhanced role of the military. Lietenant-General J.R. Dutton, SADF chief of staff operations, wrote that 'in the new perspective ... civil riots, strikes accompanied by violence and urban terrorism are seen as part of the total assault' and could not longer be left to BOSS and the SAP to deal with. Therefore:

> the military role in National Security can no longer be confined exclusively to the employment of armed force. It is

> broadened to include contributory roles in virtually every other sphere of strategic action and specifically in the psychological, economic and political spheres.[21]

The 1979 Defence White Paper provided for the establishment of a 'national strategic planning process' involving all departments and directed by the State Security Council and the Prime Minister's Department.[22]

Interestingly enough, Andreas Wassenaar (see chapter four above) was an advocate of South African adoption of the 'Brazilian model', and in particular the military regime's recruitment of ministers from the private sector, funding of private enterprise and encouragement of partnerships involving the state, local capital and multinationals.[23] Unlike Vorster, who had been infuriated by Wassenaar's book, Botha agreed with the criticisms it contained of the overinflated public sector. He encouraged Owen Horwood, the minister of finance, who had already implemented an austerity programme in 1976-77, to adopt monetarist policies designed to reduce the economic role of the state. After rising at an annual rate of ten per cent in 1973-76 real government expenditure increased by only one per cent in 1977, by half a per cent in 1978 and was static in 1979.[24] Horwood's 1980 budget, which gave away R1.5 billion to whites in tax cuts was greeted by the *Financial Mail* as giving 'substance to prime minister P.W. Botha's promises to revitalise the free market economy and switch resources to the private sector'.[25] Plans were announced to convert Sasol into a holding company owned 70 per cent by private shareholders, 30 per cent by the state.[26]

The Wiehahn and Riekert Reports

It was, however, less Botha's economic policies than his plans for rationalising apartheid that won him the support of big business. These plans were unveiled when the reports of two government commissions chaired by two of the Afrikaner intellectuals whose influence increased under Botha, were published in May 1979. The more fundamental of the two documents was the Riekert report, concerned with the machinery of influx control. The thinking behind it was spelled out by Jan Lombard in a paper already quoted:

> South Africa must 'normalise' the character of its socio-economic regime in terms of the concepts used in the great debate between the forces of individual liberty, on the one hand, and communism, on the other hand ... If, in other words, the maintenance of order requires discriminatory provisions in our legal system, these provisions must be defined in terms of other characteristics directly correlated to the maintenance of order. To declare or imply that racial difference as such are, in themselves, a threat to political order and socio-economic stability is simply no longer accepted.[27]

Apartheid, then, could no longer be justified, either to foreign opinion or indeed to the black middle class on which the regime increasingly rested its hopes, in racial terms. Indeed, P.J. Riekert, the chairman and sole commissioner (again, no liberal — he had served a spell in internment camps during the second world war along with Vorster and Van Den Bergh for supporting the pro-Nazi Ossewa Brandwag) was highly critical of aspects of the migrant labour system: the massive BAD bureaucracy and the arrest of vast numbers of Africans for minor breaches of the pass laws (278,887 in 1978 alone) had become counter-productive, helping to provoke the Soweto uprising and severely limiting the mobility of labour-power. However, Riekert did not advocate the abolition of influx control:

> Owing to the potential extent and the nature of the migration of blacks from rural areas to urban areas, serious social and sociological welfare problems would arise in urban areas in South Africa ... if the migration process is left uncontrolled ... Control over the rate of urbanisation is, in the light of circumstances in South Africa, an absolutely essential social security measure.[28]

In other words, the Bantustans should continue to perform their function of a dumping ground for 'non-productive' blacks. Riekert actually advocated tightening up influx control by making employers, rather than the Africans themselves, liable for breaches of the pass laws. This measure along with the abolition of the old rule that blacks should have to prove their right to be in a prescribed (urban) area for more than 72 hours would end the mass arrests of pass law offenders and mean that the demand for passes, Riekert told an academic audience, 'which causes so much bitterness to blacks, will not take place in public, as at present, but in the secluded office of the employer's personnel office. We must get the thing off the streets.'[29]

At the same time, Riekert abandoned his earlier opposition to the right of a minority of Africans to reside in urban areas under section 10 (1) of the Blacks (Urban Areas) Consolidation Act as 'in conflict with the accepted policy that every Bantu in South Africa belongs to a people with a political home of its own'.[30] These rights should be retained, not abolished and 'influx control should be linked only with the availability of work and of approved housing'.[31] 'Section tenners' should be guaranteed the right to have their families with them — hitherto, not always the case — and the right to move from one urban area to another provided that jobs and approved housing were available, increasing labour mobility. These proposals were based on the premise, stated explicitly by the commission on labour law chaired by Professor Nic Wiehahn, that 'black workers are a permanent part of the South African economy' and 'are no longer ... "mainly unskilled" ' but 'have achieved a fare greater degree of employment stability and industrialisation'.[32]

In line with this thinking, Wiehahn recommended that Africans should be permitted to form trade unions registered under the Industrial Conciliation Act, which, *inter alia*, makes strikes effectively illegal, bans shop stewards and the involvement of unions in political activity and has encouraged the development within the white labour movement of a trade-union bureaucracy incorporated in the state machine.[33] The commission complained that the existing unregistered black unions 'in fact enjoy much greater freedom than registered [i.e. white] unions, to the extent that they are free if they so wished to participate in politics'. The report warned that 'the influence of this extra-statutory segment could well undermine the statutory systems' and argued that permitting the registration of black trade unions:

> would have the beneficial effect of countering polarisation and ensuring a more orderly process of collective bargaining, in addition to exposing black trade unions to South

> Africa's trade-union tradition and the existing institutions, thus inculcating a sense of responsibility and loyalty towards the free market system.[34]

The *Financial Mail* commented:

> It would be wrong to dismiss either the Riekert or the Wiehahn report as merely advocating cosmetic change. The change is real — but central to both documents is the replacement of crude racial discrimination by more sophisticated techniques of control. Also central to both reports is the idea of building up a privileged labour aristocracy among blacks in the urban areas.

Sheena Duncan of the Black Sash which sought to help the victims of the pass laws was quoted as saying:

> Isolating a privileged group of blacks in the urban areas is going to take place at the expense of a vast number of people in the homelands, whose only safety net up to now has been the inefficiency of the influx control system, which has enabled them to survive by getting jobs, albeit illegally, in the informal sector of the urban areas. Now this venue will be closed to them and starvation appears to be the inevitable result.[35]

The government's initial response to the two reports narrowed the margin of change proposed. The Industrial Conciliation Amendment Act implementing Wiehahn excluded migrant and foreign workers from trade union rights, gave the government registrar wide powers to grant and withdraw registration and forbade multiracial unions.[36] As the *Financial Mail* pointed out, 'the new system is there to control, not to strengthen the unions'.[37] The government white paper on Riekert refused to scrap the 72-hour rule or to end the prosecution of blacks breaking the pass laws. However, a law was speedily passed raising the maximum fine per worker from R100 to R500 for the illegal employment of Africans. Sheena Duncan commented that these stiffer penalties for employers 'are so severe that there will be no more illegal employment'.[38] The Black Sash advice centres in Johannesburg and Cape Town were soon flooded with Africans sacked by employers fearful of the new fines and Piet Koornhof, minister of co-operation and development (as BAD is known these days) was forced to announce a moratorium until 31 October 1979 on the R500 penalty. But by the following January Sheena Duncan reported that prosecution and sackings of 'illegal' Africans were 'worse than ever before. Cases which we would expect to win five years ago are now just not succeeding'.[39]

This did not prevent the employers giving Botha their support. The president of the Transvaal Chamber of Industries, Jack Holloway, responded to the new fines by saying: 'we are in favour of influx control because it protects the entire society'.[40] And Harry Oppenheimer, patron of the liberal white opposition, had said even before Botha took office:

> I would handle influx control quite separately. I think we certainly need it in the sense of providing a service to black people, because it is certainly true that if you had no machinery for directing people to where jobs are, you would get too many swamping the urban areas, where there are neither jobs nor housing to cope with them.[41]

At the same time, the employers were given what they wanted in other respects. By the late 1970s the acute shortage of white labour and the militancy of the black working class had made imperative both the intensified rationalisation of production, which would, by deskilling labour, reduce white workers' bargaining power, and an assault on job reservation.[42] A major victory was won by the employers when an industrial council agreement involving the white unions in July 1978 opened all job categories to Africans in the crucial iron, steel, engineering and metallurgical industries. The offensive against white labour was not so peaceful in the mines where since the 1920s white workers had been able to retain significant control over the labour-process by insisting that blacks not be issued with blasting certificates, which entitled the bearer to head an underground gang (although in the rapidly expanding open-cast coal mines, where blasting was replaced by the use of walking dragline scrapers driven by Africans, the basis of white bargaining power had been undermined). Resistance to change was spearheaded by the Mine Workers Union (MWU), led by Arrie Paulus, who came to power as part of an Action Committee which had successfully blocked an 'experiment' in the 1960s by the Chamber of Mines designed to reduce the role of the white gangers.[43]

On 5 March 1979 MWU members went on strike at the American-owned O'Kiep mine at Nabapeep in protest against the transfer there of three Coloured artisans. By 7 March 7,500 white miners were on strike nationally. The MWU leadership seem to have seen this as a one-day protest action, but the Chamber of Mines decided to provoke a confrontation, scrapped the closed-shop agreement with the union and sacked the strikers. The Minister of Mines, Fanie Botha, refused to intervene and even threatened to introduce legislation banning protest strikes. The Chamber's threat to make the strikers pay an 'economic rental' of R6 a day for their company houses forced the MWU executive to call the strike off. Paulus described the government's support for the mine owners 'the biggest treason toward the white workers in white South Africa since the days in 1922 when white mine-workers were shot down in the Rand by General Smuts'.[44] Fear of a white backlash did not prevent Botha accepting Wiehahn's proposals that the statutory colour bar be scrapped (although job reservation imposed by collective agreement with registered unions or by the employer's choice was still permitted) and that the training of black apprentices in white areas be allowed.

One final ingredient of Botha's strategy also had the support of big business, and indeed had been advocated by its representatives for some time — namely, the encouragement of an urban black middle class. Separate development had blocked the achievement of an African bourgeoisie outside the Bantustans. The frustrations of the business and professional classes that did develop in the townships was well expressed by Dr Ntatho Motlana, chairman of the Soweto Committee of Ten:

> '*I* get frequently stopped in the middle of the day, in the middle of Johannesburg, in my professional safari suit — and I buy them expensive — with the words, '*Jou pas, jong*' [Your pass, man].[45]

After Soweto, both Afrikaner and English speaking capital swung behind the notion of a black middle class that would act as a buffer between the white minority and the African masses. The Urban Foundation was launched to tackle the problem of urban blacks. At its founding conference in November 1976,

Anton Rupert, head of the Afrikaner multinational Rembrandt's, said: 'a prerequisite for achieving our overall objectives should be the adoption of free enterprise values by urban blacks'.[46]

Gradually, and in the face of opposition from within the National Party and BAD, reforms were introduced to make life easier for the urban blacks, notably when in December 1978 blacks were permitted to buy 99-year leaseholds in urban areas, an admission that they were more than 'temporary sojourners' in the 'white' areas. However, by June 1979 only one such leasehold had been granted — to the Soweto millionaire Richard Maponya; financial institutions were reluctant to lend to potential African home-owners unless the latter had full ownership rights.[47] At the same time, moves began to be taken in the direction of permitting black firms to operate outside the townships and homelands. Piet Koornhof told the National African Federated Chambers of Commerce (NAFCOC) in July 1979 that 'by 1982 the black businessman would have arrived in South Africa and taken his rightful place in the economy'.[48]

However, there were real differences of interest between white and black business. Many South African industries — notably food, clothing and footwear — were basing their hopes of expansion on the growth of the African market. Already the rise in blacks' share of personal income (22.5 per cent in 1970, 25.4 per cent in 1975, 28.9 per cent in 1980) and the flight of whites to the suburbs meant that the central business districts (CBDs) were becoming more and more dependent on African consumers;[49] 44 per cent of Johannesburg CBD income (excluding the motor trade) came from blacks.[50] The director of Ford South Africa's parts and services division predicted that black car ownership would rise from 8.2 per cent in 1977 to 25 per cent nine years later.[51] He explained that:

> the white market is close to saturation point and we must look to the rest of the population for an increase in volume to the 500,000 units a year the industry requires to utilise production to its maximum and to reduce production costs.[52]

Other industries also had their eyes fixed on the African market, which some economists expected to account for half the total spending by the end of the 1980s. Thus the electrification of Soweto, financed by government and private loans, would lead, according to the *Financial Mail*, to 'a mini-boom in black spending in consumer durables'.[53] The 6,000 black retailers in the townships were, not unreasonably, afraid that this market would be snapped up by the big white-owned chain stores. NAFCOC demanded protection against 'unfair competition' and a monopoly of trading in the townships. This did not prevent plans being made to establish a CBD at Jabulani in Soweto, in which a number of big retailers — Checkers/Greatermans, Southern Sun, Ster Kniekor — showed an interest, despite the protest of African businessmen.

At no point did either the government or big business consider extending the economic concessions they had offered to significant political reforms. Jan Lombard, one of the theorists of the new strategy, wrote:

> The replacement of colour discrimination by classical norms of competition and democracy in the production and distribution of goods and services, both in the private and the public sector, does not automatically imply the subjugation of the sovereignty of the state to the whims of simple majorities in the total population ... Under present circumstances, that would be tantamount to the destruction of all freedom in southern Africa.[54]

Proposals were published in May 1980 for the establishment of separate parliaments for whites, Coloured and Asians, each of which would be represented on a President's Council with a white chairman (Alwyn Schlebusch, author of these proposals, was nominated for the post). Africans, however, would be excluded from this 'dispensation'. The homeland leaders would form a separate council, while the townships would be conceded greater powers of self-government within the framework of the Community Councils Act 1977. In the meantime, neither Afrikanerdom nor English-speaking capital would even consider black people's basic demand — universal suffrage. Here again, the difference between the 'liberal' capitalist Harry Oppenheimer, and Broederbond chairman Gerrit Viljoen was very slight. Oppenheimer said:

> It may well be that we should have Soweto organised on a canton or several cantons and that they should govern themselves in the local sense and then should be represented in some central parliament.[55]

This did not seem so far from Viljoen's concession that:

> in the long run certain black areas, such as the large complexes of the Witwatersrand, will in the long run have to attain some sort of city state independence ... Through separation one could develop a confederal system, which in time to come could develop into a federal one and maybe in the next century into a union.[56]

The Limits of Change

In the course of 1979 euphoria steadily built up in white business circles about Botha's new course. In contrast to the inertia of Vorster's later years here seemed a leader who was ready to push through the reforms necessary to stabilise South African capitalism. Botha unveiled a 12-point programme for change at the Natal congress of the Nationalist party, defended his policies before a hostile audience at the Transvaal congress and told Afrikaners to 'adapt or die'. His Minister of Co-operation and Development, Piet Koornhof, a former chief secretary of the Broederbond, even claimed, in Miami of all places, that 'apartheid as the world knew it is dead'. The high point came when Botha and his cabinet met 250 businessmen at the five-star Carlton hotel in Johannesburg on 22 November 1979. This meeting — Botha's 'most spectacular coup since reaching the premiership', the *Financial Mail* called it — saw Harry Oppenheimer give the government his critical support.[57] Botha's aim seemed to be to isolate, and if necessary force out, the Nationalist far right, at the same time drawing English-speaking capital behind him.

There followed a series of major setbacks for Botha. In February 1980 he seemed all set to sack Andries Treurnicht, the chief hardliner in the cabinet, who had succeeded Connie Mulder as leader of the Transvaal Nationalists, but occupied the minor government post of Minister of Public Works, Statistics and Tourism. At the last moment, Botha backed off in the face of opposition within the cabinet and caucus. Vorster emerged from retirement to denounce him, and the victory of ZANU-PF in Zimbabwe delivered an apparently fatal blow to his plan to create a 'constellation of states' dominated by Pretoria in southern Africa.

The basis for resistance to reforms could be counted under three heads. First, there was the opposition within the National Party itself. Although the initiative lay firmly in the hands in the cabinet, whose proposals the parliamentary caucus normally accepted;

> power has come increasingly to rest on a provincial rather than an ideological base. The provincial parties have become personal fiefdoms of their respective leaders, with enormous patronage, including cabinet posts, at their disposal as well as the power to protect followers.[58]

The Transvaal party, whose MPs were in any case more *verkrampte* than the rest of the caucus,[59] were infuriated by their loss of the premiership in September 1978. Treurnicht had their support less as the upholder of unmitigated apartheid than as the standard-bearer of Transvaal interests within the Nationalist establishment. The *Financial Mail* reported after Vorster's fall that 'party divisions are now grouped along party lines — Transvaal versus the rest'.[60] The Transvaal congress in September 1980 cheered Treurnicht when he declared that 'any political planning aimed at getting white and black nations to grow together politically or socially is unacceptable to whites' and gave Botha a rough ride when he spoke. As *The Times* put it, the congress 'regards him as a Cape Nationalist leader who is a temporary tenant of the premier political position'.[61]

The second focus of opposition lay in the bureaucracy centred around BAD (now the Department of Co-operation and Development):

> Verwoerd [as minister of native affairs in the 1950s] embarked on the elaboration of the apartheid policy and the creation of a vast bureaucratic structure. Just before he became prime minister in 1958 he was under fire within the party for creating 'an empire of unprecedented scale out of his own department — a state within a state'. Verwoerd more than any other prime minister before or after him imbued the bureaucracy with his particular political vision. 'He attracted not pliable servants but like-minded ideologues', a top bureaucrat who worked in close association with him would later recount ... Today the apartheid bureaucracy is staffed mainly by men dedicated to the

ideology of separate development. They form the resident opposition in the National Party to any attempts at reforms of the Verwoerdian blueprint.[62]

The white civil service, with a vested interest in the maintenance of apartheid, and enjoying the advantage of knowing their way around the vast network of statutes and regulations created by the Nationalist regime, were a formidable obstacle to change, resisting every reform, and taking full advantage of the cabinet's method of modifying apartheid through administrative actions rather than amendments of the law.

Finally, there was the white working class. Afrikaners in particular are entrenched within the public sector. In 1977 30 per cent of economically active whites were employed in this sector — 35 per cent of Afrikaners as opposed to 25 per cent of English speakers, who occupy only 10 per cent of the top positions.[63] White public sector employees, guaranteed well-paid jobs by successive Nationalist governments, would obviously resist any attempt to introduce large number of Africans. In general, white workers were being squeezed. Their wages were rising more slowly than those of blacks while they were vulnerable to the employers' offensive. Women — their proportion of the white workforce was expected to rise from 29 per cent in 1969 to 37 per cent in 1981, no less than 83 per cent of them working in nursing, teaching and clerical and sales jobs — would be especially likely to suffer with the rationalisation of office work (the value of computer equipment installed rose by 55 per cent in the 18 months to mid-1979).[64]

White workers were in no sense the autonomous initiators of racial oppression South Africa, as some bourgeois commentators have claimed.[65] In general, they accepted political subordination to the Afrikaner bourgeoisie and petty bourgeoisie in exchange for economic privileges within the framework of South Africa's 'racially exclusive bourgeois democracy'. Arthur Grobelaar, leader of the main white trade union federation, TUCSA, expressed the class-collaborationist politics of the white labour movement when he said: 'Co-operation with management is the crux of industrial relations. I hope TUCSA unions are collaborating with management. This falls within the ambit of partnership in industry'.[66] Even the far-right Confederation of Labour rather grudgingly accepted the Wiehahn report, despite the opposition of the MWU. Nevertheless, as the government aligned itself more closely to a capitalist class engaged in the erosion of white economic privileges, a white backlash could not be ruled out. Disgruntled white miners voted for the ultra-*verkramp* HNP in a series of by-elections in 1979, and the Transvaalse Onderwysersvereniging, 'the most powerful body of teachers in South Africa', threatened to go on strike if Treurnicht was sacked.

For support Botha could rely on the military and big business, both English-speaking and Afrikaans. His problem lay in the narrowness of his popular base among Afrikaners. In response to opposition within the National Party, he sought to detach the executive from parliamentary control, moving towards what a senior government MP called 'a civilian-military junta'.[67] This involved in part the 'coalition government with private enterprise' advocated by Wassenaar.[68] In June 1979 Botha appointed some business leaders, notably Dick Goss of South African Breweries and Wim de Villiers of General Mining, to the Public Service Commission in an effort to streamline the administration and break down bureaucratic obstruction. The constitution was changed to permit the appointment of ministers from outside parliament. This move was followed by a cabinet reshuffle in August 1980, which brought General Magnus Malan and Gerrit Viljoen into the government as ministers of defence and of national education respectively. It was only then that Botha felt confident enough to press ahead with implementing the Riekert report. Proposals linking influx control to the availability of jobs and housing and scrapping the 72-hour rule were published in October 1980.

One of Malan's generals had written in 1978:

> Two requirements for the application of total strategy would appear to favour a system of unified command, joint central planning, decentralised execution and sustained vertical and horizontal organisation ... Conventional organisations in democratic systems do not as a rule lend themselves to these procedures. Therefore organisational changes or adaptations would appear to be imperative.[69]

Was Botha moving towards an 'exceptional state' which would dispense with the need for securing the consent of even the white population? The conditions for such a '*verligte* dictatorship' certainly existed — a crisis of ruling-class hegemony, serious divisions within the power bloc, a serious challenge from the popular masses.[70] Yet there were perhaps insuperable obstacles on the road to such an 'exceptional state'. Short of a military coup, impossible because it might involve armed conflict between whites which could provoke a successful black uprising, there seemed no easy way to remove the Nationalist opponents of change in parliament and the bureaucracy. They remained well entrenched: Gerrit Viljoen was replaced as chairman of the Broederbond by Carel Boshoff, author of a preposterous plan to preserve the purity of apartheid by setting up a white 'homeland' in the eastern Cape. Attempts to fuse Afrikaner and English-speaking interests had led to the political destruction of earlier Afrikaner leaders — Jan Smuts and J.B.M. Hertzog. Such might be Piet Botha's fate.

In any case, Botha's aim was to rationalise apartheid, not abolish it. The proposals of the Wiehahn and Riekert commissions were designed to adjust the system of influx control to the needs of South African capitalism in the 1980s. These needs involved demand for more differentiated forms of black labour — to the old roles of unskilled contract labourer (still crucial in industries such as mining and textiles) and semi-skilled operative were added those of skilled worker, technician and even foreman. The division at the heart of Riekert between section-tenners and migrants was designed to provide a more flexible system of labour control and supply that would be capable of responding to these needs. Influx control would remain at its basis, both as a 'social security measure' to shunt the unemployed off to the Bantustans and as a means of moulding the black workforce to capital's needs. Neither it nor the white monopoly of political power were regarded by Botha as negotiable. *Pace* Piet 'Promises' Koornhof, apartheid was far from dead.

6. The Third Round — Workers and Students Challenge Botha

Far more serious than any divisions in the white camp was the wave of strikes and student boycotts which shook South Africa in mid-1980. For the third time in less than a decade large-scale popular struggles erupted, challenging the system of white supremacy. There had been the Durban mass strikes in 1973 and the Soweto uprising of 1976. This time school boycotts in the Cape came together with an outburst of black industrial militancy.

The White Economy Revives

The context of this new upsurge was provided by the recovery of the South African economy from what Andreas Wassenaar called 'the most severe financial and economic crisis that it has ever known'.[1] The 1976-77 recession was followed by two sluggish years: real gross domestic product rose by 2½ per cent in 1978, 3¾ per cent in 1979.[2] The stimulus for growth came from abroad. South Africa's integration in the world economy means that its trade cycle follows that of western Europe and the United States, with a time lag varying between 6 and 12 months in the former's case, 9 and 15 months in the latter's.[3] The slow and uncertain recovery of the world capitalist economy from the 1974-75 recession underlay South Africa's stagnation. When help came it reflected the weakness of the international system.

The US Treasury exploited the economic and political turmoil of the mid-1970s, and the short-lived American balance of payments surplus in 1975, to force the International Monetary Fund to agree to the demonetisation of gold. A major step had already been taken in this direction in August 1971, when the Nixon administration suspended the convertibility of the dollar into gold. The idea was to persuade the rest of the western block to finance US balance of payments deficits, a product of American capitalism's declining competitive position relative to the EEC and Japan, by accepting dollars even though these were no longer backed by gold. Washington's temporary victory in the monetary war at Jamaica in 1975, when the IMF agreed to sell off one-sixth of its gold reserves as a first step towards depriving the metal of any monetary role, pushed the price of gold down from a peak of just under $200 per ounce at the end of 1974 to barely $100 eighteen months later and precipitated the South African recession.[4]

It was, similarly, the blunting of the American offensive which laid the basis for South Africa's recovery. The US economic revival of the late 1970s, feeble though it was by post-war standards, pushed up the inflation rate and sucked in imports of oil and manufactured goods. The resulting balance of payments deficit, combined with the Carter administration's hamfisted attempt to 'talk down' the dollar and thus make American goods more competitive, pushed the dollar down and gold up. A number of other factors helped to encourage the rise in the gold price — in particular, the movement of Arab oil producers' funds out of the dollar into other currencies and gold, and the decision by EEC to back the new European currency unit (ECU) partly with gold. But at the beginning of 1979 the gold price stood only at $225 an ounce. Then came what the *Economist* called 'one of the most remarkable comebacks in post-war history'.[5] The continued shift of OPEC funds into gold pushed the price sharply upwards and forced the US Treasury to admit defeat and abandon its sales of gold in November 1979. Panic caused by the Soviet occupation of Afghanistan led to a peak gold price of $835 an ounce on 18 January 1980; even after the price fell back in March, it stabilised at a level of about $650 an ounce. The *Economist* commented:

> Behind the speculative froth was a fundamental change in the way people think about gold. No longer was it regarded as an exotic investment but as something that might remain as a store of value when paper currencies were suspect. What made 1979 conspicuously different from previous gold flurries was that the metal appreciated not

> only in dollar terms but against other currencies as well — even the Swiss franc. The strength of gold was a mirror image of the world's loss of faith in all major currencies.[6]

The result was that central banks' inclination to retain or purchase gold as a reserve asset increased markedly. This trend, combined with suggestions that the metal be used in international settlements,[7] signified that gold was resuming monetary functions usurped by the dollar, and amounted to 'the complete collapse of the attempts by US imperialism to impose a "demonetarisation" of gold, to stabilise a "world monetary system" based upon depreciating paper-dollars'.[8] Fundamental factors — the continued economic decline of American capitalism, the existence of several hundred billion dollars held outside any national monetary system, falling gold production (the Chamber of Mines estimates that South African output in 2000 will be half that in 1978)[9] — made it likely that the supply of gold would be less than the demand, and that its price would therefore in the long term continue to rise.

The rising gold price implied a radical improvement in South Africa's economic prospects. The value of the country's gold sales rose by nearly 50 per cent in 1979, helping to push up minerals' share of total exports from 68 to 73 per cent.[10] One economist declared euphorically:

> if the gold price stabilises at $500 and South Africa sells 700 tonnes a year, annual earnings from gold alone will be nearly $11,000 million. The country could thrive for a decade. South Africa would be like an OPEC country.[11]

The soaring gold price made it easier for South Africa to borrow abroad. The *Financial Times* reported in August 1980:

> South Africa is poised to undertake a $250m financing in the Euromarkets. The credit marks a significant step towards the rehabilitation of the country as a respectable international borrower, largely because it is being handled with much less discretion than is normally the case for Euromarket burrowings by this country ... Now, however, the banks are beginning to accept that the country is set on a gradual relaxation of apartheid. At the same time they are aware that the rapid rise in the gold price over the past two years makes the country a first-class credit risk.[12]

At the same time, South Africa's dependence on exports and foreign capital had been somewhat reduced by the completion of the vast investment projects of the 1970s, which both reduced the demands for foreign loans and imports, and enhanced South Africa's capacity to export.

Better economic prospects encouraged a rapid expansion in investment, which had fallen in real terms during the second half of the 1970s. By February 1980 the *Financial Mail* was reporting a 'capital spending spree' in both public and private sectors. In part this reflected a recovery in profitability — the real rate of return on capital in 1978 was 8.4 per cent, low by historical standards but still up on the very depressed level (between 2 and 3 per cent) reached in 1976.[14] There were other factors at work as well — capital spending in the gold mines during the 1980s, stimulated by the high price, was likely to equal everything spent on them up to that time. The 1979 oil crisis hit South Africa, which had hitherto relied on oil imports from Iran, especially hard, forcing the regime to buy on the spot market at $35-40 a barrel and encouraging the expansion of the Sasol coal-into-oil project and of coal- and nuclear-powered electricity generating capacity; import substitution was encouraged by strategic arguments (e.g. synthetic rubber, diesel engines) and, in the case of the car industry, the requirement that 66 per cent of the content of vehicles assembled in South Africa must be locally produced. An expected 5 per cent rise in real fixed investment in 1980,[15] combined with a sharp rise in white consumer spending ('the extra liquidity Horwood will be pouring into taxpayers' pockets after the budget is a virtual invitation to lash out in a spending spree', said the *Financial Mail*),[16] made likely 6 per cent real growth, a substantial improvement on the 1.5 per cent annual average in 1975-79.[17]

... And So Does The Black Labour Movement

'Blacks are seldom more than ghosts at Mr. Horwood's budget feasts', the *Economist* commented.[18] In April 1979 less than half the households in Soweto earned the housing subsistence level (HSL), an estimate of the basic survival level for an African family of five, of R159.76 a month.[19] Economic recovery pushed up inflation, which in any case remained in double figures even at the depth of the recession. In August

1979 food prices were rising at an annual rate of 16.8 per cent, while transport costs had risen in the previous year by 53 per cent.[20] In the six months to November 1979 the HSL rose 13.3 per cent in Durban, 13 per cent in Germiston, 12.2 per cent in Bloemfontein, 11.5 per cent in Peddie and Boksburg.[21] Seven out of ten cases admitted to the pediatric department at Baragwanath hospital in Soweto suffered from malnutrition.[22] And workers in the cities were, on the whole, better off than those in the Bantustans. Men and women working on a coffee plantation in the 'independent' state of Venda were paid a maximum of respectively R23.00 and R16.00 a month.[23] Infant mortality in the Transkei was 282 per 1000 — more than twice that of India (122 per 1000).[24] A study of black housing suggested that Riekert's proposal to make influx control dependent in part on the availability of suitable housing was something of a sick joke. The black housing backlog outside the homelands was over 200,000 units and would cost R1 billion to eliminate. There were 350,000 black squatters in Durban, 250,000 at Winterveld, in Bophuthatswana near Pretoria, another 265,000 blacks in substandard conditions in Pietermaritzburg. Given that the urban population was likely to rise from 11.5 million to 25.5 million by the year 2000, some four million additional black houses would be required.[25] Yet black housing starts in the 'white' areas fell from 14,369 in 1968 to 6,109 in 1977.[26] The waiting list for a rented house in Soweto was nine years.[27] Stricter enforcement of the pass laws and the introduction of a R500 fine on employers meant that the yoke of apartheid was tightening around black people's necks, not relaxing.

Table 14 lists some of the major disputes in 1979-80. As can be seen, union recognition and victimisation loom large in the issues sparking off disputes. This reflected the offensive launched by employers, white unions and the state against the embryonic black labour movement in the wake of the Wiehahn report. The changes in the labour law occasioned by this report encouraged attacks on the black unions. As we have seen, the new legislation was highly restrictive, designed to place African trade unions within the straitjacket of 'industrial conciliation'. A survey of 200 companies revealed that three-fifths were opposed to African trade unions, half would prefer to deal with no union at all, while 90 per cent wished to deal with their

African workers at the plant level within the framework of government-sponsored liaison and works committees (retained under the new law).[29] The employers' tough line was reflected in guidelines issued by the powerful Steel and Engineering Industries Federation of South Africa (SEIFSA) instructing its members to have no dealings with black trade unions that had not received final registration, to deny them recruitment and publicity facilities, and to continue to use works and liaison committees to negotiate with their African employees.[30] SEIFSA's director-general, Erroll Drummond, had sat on the Wiehahn commission, and had opposed the extension of trade union rights to migrant workers and commuters from the Bantustans.[31]

The employers enjoyed the full support and co-operation of one of the main white trade-union federations, the Trade Union Council of South Africa (TUCSA), whose response to the Wiehahn report was to establish a committee to organise African workers. Their strategy was to form black 'parallel unions' linked to, and controlled by, a parent white union. One such parallel union had existed for many years — the National Union of Clothing Workers headed by Lucy Mvubelo, which joined TUCSA when it decided to admit African unions (after having been twice expelled previously) in the early 1970s. According to the *Financial Mail*, the NUCW was kept firmly under the thumb of its white 'parent', the Garment Workers Union of South Africa, whose secretary, Senator Anna Scheepers, 'virtually vetoes NUCW decisions if she does not approve of them' and 'calls in the executive and lectures them like grade schoolchildren and then tells them to go back and reconsider'.[32] After Wiehahn, and faced with an employers' offensive against white workers aimed at replacing them with cheaper Africans, TUCSA decided to organise their potential rivals, and thus to control their activities. In most cases the parallel's general secretary was that of the white 'parent'. One TUCSA leader defended this practice with these words:

> You mean to tell me that we are going to pay R10,000 and let them do what they bloody well like? ... We haven't spent all this money just that they should run away with it themselves and start becoming friends of the ANC, oh no, when I am secretary then that union does what I say.[33]

Table 14: Disputes involving black workers, April 1979 - August 1980

Date	Firm	Number involved	Union	Comment
April 1979	Elandsrand Mine (Anglo American)	4500	—	Riot on eve of mine's opening.
May-Nov. 1979	Fatti's & Moni's, Bellville (W. Cape)	80	FCWU	Victimisation/Union recognition (see text).
Aug. 1979	Rainbow Chickens, Hammersdale	—	FOSATU	Strike started by sacking of woman trade-union activist. 55 workers arrested after police teargas mass meeting. Strikers replaced with casual labour, but after production falls some of the original workers taken on again.
Nov. 1979 -Jan. 1980	Ford, General Tire & Rubber, Port Elizabeth	2,000	UAW	Victimisation (see text).
Dec. 1979	Cape docks	400-600	WPGWU	Union recognition. Successful.
Dec. 1979	Sea Harvest Fish Factory, Saldhana Bay (W. Cape)	600	FCWU	Strike for R30 per week minimum wage (current minimum R20-50, average R32). Partial success.
Jan. 1980	Unilever, Boksburg		Black Food & Beverage Workers	Steward victimised.
Feb. 1980	CMGM civil engineering site, Saldhana Bay		WPGWU	Victimisation of eight workers.
Feb. 1980	Ceres Fruit-growers Co-op (W. Cape)	750	FCWU	Victimisation during wage negotiations.

Date	Firm	Number involved	Union	Comment
May-Aug 1980	Cape Town meat industry (18 factories)		WPGWU	Union recognition. Defeated after union organisers arrested.
May 1980	Frame textile group, Durban Pinetown	7,000	NUTW	20-25 per cent wage increase demanded (see text).
June-July 1980	Volkswagen and 10 other factories, Uitenhage	7,500	UAW	Wage increase (see text).
July 1980	Johannesburg buses	1,000		15 per cent wage increase won.
July 1980	Sasol construction site, Secunda	18,000		(see text)
July-Aug. 1980	Johannesburg Municipality	10,000	BMWU	Wages/union recognition (see text).

The formation of parallel unions was encouraged by management in order to block the growth of the independent black unions. Thus Leyland South Africa, which had resisted recognising the unregistered Metal and Allied Workers Union since 1973, invited a coloured TUCSA union, the Motor Industry Combined Workers Union, to form a parallel for Africans at its Elandsfontein plant. The new union issued a recruiting pamphlet stating 'employers are with this union'. In general the parallels presented themselves as unions opposed to confrontation with management, stressing instead the funeral benefits they could offer members. One black worker commented, 'these unions look after us when we are dead. When we are alive they do nothing for us'.[34]

The independent black workers' movement confronting this challenge was divided both politically and geographically (see Table 15). There were three main groups — the Federation of South African Trade Unions (FOSATU), with support in Natal, the Transvaal and the eastern Cape; the Consultative Committee of Black Trade Unions, based in Johannesburg; and two loosely linked independent unions in the western Cape, the Western Province General Workers Union (WPGWU) and Food and Canning Workers Union (FCWU). White activists, largely drawn from left-wing English-speaking students and academics, many of them radicalised through their participation in the anti-apartheid National Union of South African Students (NUSAS), played an important role in the formation of FOSATU and the WPGWU, both of which were multiracial. The Consultative Committee, by contrast, influenced by the black consciousness movement, was highly critical of the leading role played by whites in FOSATU — for example, its general secretary, Alec Irwin. However, a rather more right-wing group of white advisers, the Urban Training Project, had played an important part in the formation of the Consultative Committee unions. FOSATU was probably the most important of the three groups, and was formed in April 1979, when a number of Consultative Committee unions split away to join up with the Natal-based Trade Union Advisory and Co-ordinating Council, founded in October 1973 in the wake of the mass strikes.

FOSATU and the WPGWU were divided on tactics. The latter were committed to building a general union as the framework within which workers could build their own rank-and-file controlled plant committees. FOSATU, by contrast, advocated industrial unions and demanded recognition from the employers. All the black unions, even the parallel NUCW, refused to register under the new Industrial Conciliation Act as long as migrants and commuters were denied trade-union rights. The significance of this issue can be measured by the fact that the number of commuters, living in Bantustans but working in 'white' areas, had risen from 290,000 to 637,000 between 1970 and 1977.[35] It was government policy to encourage commuting, often by attaching black townships to Bantustans. The Deputy Minister of Co-operation and Development, Ferdie Hartzengerg, said: 'if blacks live in their own country and travel on a daily basis to South Africa, then the political problem would be solved'. Commuters' earnings amounted to nearly a quarter of the Bantustans' gross national income.[36] The two main Durban townships, Kwamashu and Umlazi, had been made part of the Kwazulu homeland: thus, if the law were strictly applied, Durban, the heart of FOSATU, would have been cut out of the black labour movement. Eighty per cent of the WPGWU's membership were contract workers, reflecting the widespread use of African migrant labour in the western Cape.[37] In September 1979 the government backed down in the face of the black unions' anger and conceded union rights to migrants and commuters.

Table 15: South African Trade Unions

Name	No. of Unions	Membership			
		African	Coloured/ Asian	White	Total
Consultative Committee of Black Trade Unions	9	33,000			33,000
Co-ordinating Committee of TU (a)	12			28,000	28,000
FOSATU	13	48,000	12,000		60,000
SA Confederation of Labour (b)	22			179,700	179,700
TUCSA (c)	59	21,122	171,747	59,865	252,734
SACTU (d)					
Unaffiliated (e)					
registered unions	81		57,000	184,500	241,500
Total	196	102,122	240,747	452,065	794,934

(a) Ten of these unions are also affiliated to the Confederation. Most are non-salaried employees of provincial and municipal councils.
(b) 176,728 of their membership are state employees — SAR&H, SASOL, ISCOR.
(c) 7 of the 59 are African unions, 19 are Coloured and Asian only, 23 are mixed, 10 are white only.
(d) SACTU exists chiefly in exile and is affiliated to the ANC.
(e) Whites in building societies, ESCOM, underground (mines), banks. Coloured and Asian from SAR&H, municipal, industrial and service unions.

Source: R.S. Nyameko, 'Trade union movement at the cross-roads', *African Communist* No. 82, third quarter 1980, pp.30, 31.

The move, however, brought divisions over tactics to the surface. The WPGWU, backed by the Food and Canning Workers Union, argued that the law still violated 'two non-negotiable principles — the right of workers to join unions of their choice and control by workers over every aspect of their unions' activities'[38] and therefore refused to register. Both FOSATU and the Consultative Committee found themselves, however, under great pressure to register. Two FOSATU unions — the registered coloured National Union of Motor Assembly and Rubber Workers (NUMARWOSA) and the African United Automobile and Rubber Workers Union (UAW) held secret ballots on registration.[39] The FOSATU central committee, clearly worried about the TUCSA drive to build registered black parallel unions, decided that 'we would be sacrificing the best interest of all workers if we were to surrender our present role as a representative voice of integrity and allow the voice of expediency to dominate'[40] and applied, not for provisional registration, which made unions subject to all the obligations but few of the benefits of legal recognition, but for full registration. The disagreement arose in part from the much more established position of FOSATU which had succeeded in winning over NUMARWOSA (whose parallel the black UAW effectively was), while in the western Cape the WPGWU concentrated on organising African contract workers and found itself in conflict with highly conservative white and coloured artisan unions. Moreover, the political tradition of the Cape left (heavily influenced by trotskyism both directly and through the Unity Movement) involved a strong stress on the principle of boycotting apartheid institutions. The role of FOSATU in the Ford strike, however, suggests that slightly more was involved.

Confrontation at Ford[41]

The Port Elizabeth-Uitenhage conurbation in the eastern Cape, the main centre of the South African motor industry, was shaken by two major strikes in less than 12 months, at Ford from November 1979 to January 1980 and then at Volkswagen in July 1980. A variety of factors underlay the first, and far the more important, of the strikes. The depressed condition of the car industry led in July 1979 to 300 redundancies and the imposition of short-time working, as a result of which the earnings of hourly-paid African and coloured workers fell way below the household subsistence level. The 700 black workers at the Cortina assembly plant at Struandale, Port Elizabeth, were younger and better educated than those at the neighbouring engine plant; they lived in an area where the African National Congress had been strong and where the school revolt had continued into 1978. They were therefore more sensitive to Ford's lackadaisical implementation of its promises of black advancement, which had been extracted by anti-apartheid groups in the United States. They were also out of sympathy with the unregistered African United Automobile and Rubber Workers Union (UAW), which had concentrated its attention on the management-controlled liaison committee rather than shopfloor organisation. They were more sympathetic to the Port Elizabeth Black Civic Organisation (PEBCO), whose opening rally at New Brighton township on 30 October 1979 was attended by 9,000 people. The principal issue confronting the new group was the government decision to demolish another Port Elizabeth township, Walmer, and move its residents to Zwide, 22 kilometres from their jobs. But on 31 October the Cortina plant came out on strike after Thozamile Botha, a trainee industrial engineer who was also president of PEBCO, was sacked.

The strikers stayed away for three days initially. Then 200 white members of the Yster-en-Staal Unie at Ford threatened to go on strike because black workers had been paid for the time they were on strike and were 'abusing' integrated toilet and canteen facilities. African workers retaliated by walking out briefly and boycotting the canteen. The boycott spread to the nearby General Tire and Rubber plant, where 1,200 black workers walked out on 19 November after two of their number had been sacked. Two days later 600 Africans at the Ford Cortina plant followed them out on strike and were dismissed by the management, which at one stage had called in ten van- and three truck-loads of riot police. The disputes at General Tire and Rubber, and at another Port Elizabeth factory, Adamas Paper Mill, were settled quite quickly after management victories. At Ford, however, the strike dragged on until 9 January, when the management conceded the workers' main demands. The next day Thozamile Botha was arrested at a protest rally in

Walmer; the police — who had arrested over twenty of the Ford strikers in December and charged them under the Riotous Assemblies Act — were forced to use teargas, first to disperse the rally and then against a crowd that gathered after Botha had been arrested. He was eventually released, but placed under a restriction order, and fled to Lesotho in May 1980.

The Ford strike encapsulated many of the contradictions inherent in South African society. There were the growing frustrations of white workers. Henry Ferreira, assistant general secretary of the Yster-en-Staal Unie, said: 'Before Wiehahn there tended to be a lack of interest in the union of the part of white workers. Now they are more interested and more interested in joining up'.[42] The Yster-en-Staal Unie was, like the Mine Workers Union, an 'exclusive industrial union', recruiting whites irrespective of their skills, and one of the strongholds of Afrikaner nationalism in the white labour movement. From its base in the state-owned ISCOR it had expanded aggressively into the private sector. However, the process of deskilling and fragmentation was especially advanced in the metal industries, making the union more and more dependent on the state for protection. Wiehahn underlined its vulnerability.[43] At the same time, management in different firms adopted different tactics towards the black unions: General Tire and Rubber refused to have anything to do with the UAW, which had the support of most of the strikers there; Ford, on the other hand, quickly recognised the UAW and in September 1980 conceded full-time facilities to its shop stewards.

Most significant, however, were the tensions between the UAW and PEBCO. Freddie Sauls of the UAW's coloured affiliate NUMARWOSA said that the first 'walkout was not connected with a work-related problem' and that the two unions 'were not in any way connected with the walkout'.[44] The union throughout the strike operated as a fire brigade, trying again and again to persuade the workers to go back to work. George Manaase of the UAW refused to allow Thozamile Botha to address a mass meeting, said that he and PEBCO were trying to undermine the union, that the strike was 'political' and that 'we are only prepared to fight for members who approach the union'.[45] On 5 December Sauls appealed to the strikers to return to work: 'so that his union could put pressure on Ford from the inside ... the workers were stronger inside the plant'.[46] This argument was belied by the fact the eventual settlement was immediately preceded by a rally at which PEBCO (which was pulling 10,000 people to its meetings) called a boycott of white business until the strikers were reinstated. PEBCO, which had links with both the banned African National Congress (Port Elizabeth is a traditional ANC stronghold) and the black-consciousness Azanian African People's Organisation (AZAPO), enjoyed the support of the mass of the strikers — many Ford workers wore PEBCO insignia inside the plant. The union found itself outflanked when the strikers elected their own Ford Workers Committee, dominated by PEBCO activists, to run the dispute. Thozamile Botha told an interviewer:

> At one stage it [the UAW] wanted to negotiate only for union members. However, they refused to be set apart from the other workers. The union doesn't want to involve itself in politics. I don't agree with that. The position of blacks in factories is political. So the problem is also a political one, which the union cannot divorce itself from.[47]

As one commentator observed:

> one should not gauge FOSATU's attitude ... from the actions of the UAW alone, but the UAW is an important member of FOSATU, with a membership of well over 10,000 spread all over South Africa and these statements have gone unrepudiated. This [i.e. the UAW's] attitude to politics seems to command support within FOSATU as a whole.

Indeed, in December 1979 the FOSATU-affiliated Metal and Allied Workers Union (MAWU) agreed effectively to act as the white Boilermakers' Society's parallel. The latter, an artisan union, had its status challenged by the 1978 agreement to abolish job reservation in the metal industries. Its response was to seek multiracial status to enable it to recruit skilled Africans, while leaving the lower grades to MAWU. FOSATU's complaisance in this arrangement belied its commitment to multiracial industrial unions.[48]

The Cape of Storms

One of the most striking features of the 1979-80 upsurge was its geographical diversity. Thus the struggles in the western Cape reflected the very distinctive political and economic set-up in the region. The western Cape had been declared a 'coloured preference area' in 1972 — a measure designed to satisfy the claim of coloured people for political rights. The Cape National Party made the cause of the coloureds — whom they regarded as 'brown Afrikaners', sharing the language, religion and blood of the white *volk* — their own. This attitude was to some degree reciprocated — when P.W. Botha's election as National party leader was announced outside the Senate House in Cape Town, he was cheered by a mainly coloured crowd. The government, however, rejected the Theron commission's proposal that coloureds representation be given in parliament: any improvement in their position would be within the framework of separate development. A Broederbond document advocated 'separate regional economies whereby coloured people can benefit in a geographical context' which would 'eventually develop into coloured conurbations where the glories of first-class citizenship unfold for them' — coloured Bantustans, in other words.[49]

The notion of a 'coloured preference area' implied discrimination against Africans. Pieter Botha, before becoming prime minister, was able to veto the *verkrampte* Connie Mulder's proposal that African leasehold rights be extended to the western Cape.[50] In August 1978 he proposed a resolution at the Cape Nationalist congress calling for prohibitive minimum fines of employers of illegal Africans, the immediate repatriation of such workers, levies to make Africans more expensive to employ, and the prevention of the recruitment of Africans if there was coloured unemployment. Pressure from western Cape MPs, who met regularly with ministers, underlay the tough line initially taken by the regime towards the black squatters' camp at Crossroads near Cape Town. However, in April 1979, in the face of an international uproar, co-operation and development minister Piet Koornhof called off the deportation of Crossroads residents and subsequently declared the camp a township. However, the following month levies on employers of Africans in the western Cape were increased by 40 per cent, in line with the Cape Nationalists' demands. In September 1979 the Western Cape Administriation Board concluded that 18,000 out of the 24,000 residents of Crossroads were 'totally and unacceptably illegal' in the Cape peninsula and should be repatriated.[51] A wave of deportations from the western Cape followed. Seventy per cent of the African workers in the Cape were migrant labourers on short-term contracts,[52] while coloured workers, many of them in registered unions affiliated to TUSCA, tended to occupy the more skilled jobs. The opposition of a majority of employers to the coloured preference policy[53] reflected the labour-intensive character of the western Cape economy, which is concentrated in sectors such as consumer non-durables (fruit and wine) and semi-durables (clothing) and therefore dependent on plentiful cheap labour. In practice the policy encouraged firms to employ African migrants.

The regime's divide-and-rule strategy was unsuccessful. Other aspects of separate development had the effect of alienating the coloureds. In Cape Town they were moved from inner-city areas such as District Six (where in place of homes a white polytechnic was built) and dumped in townships built on a row of desolate sand-dunes known as the Cape Flats, from which their daily transport costs were as much as R1, when once they had been able to walk to work. Botha, frustrated in his attempts to pack the elected Coloured Representative Council (CRC) with his supporters, decided to replace it with an appointed council, while their participation in the CRC discredited the anti-apartheid Coloured Labour Party in the mass of the young. Faced with poverty and violence (Groote Schuur hospital is said to treat more stab wounds than any other in the world except one in New Orleans)[54] it is hardly surprising that coloured youth, especially came to see themselves as black, part of the oppressed majority. The proximity of the coloured townships on the Cape Flats to Langa, Nyanga and Guguletu, the three main African townships, probably helped to instil a sense of black unity. In 1976 coloured students and workers in the western Cape lent their support to the uprising begun by Africans in Soweto.

'In the western Cape ... over the past year, there has been a marked escalation of strikes', the *Financial Mail* noted in May 1980. There were two features of these strikes: first, they 'mainly involve unskilled and contract labour', second, the trend was 'towards rising solidarity among workers, not only among those working for the same employer but also between coloured and Africans'.[55] Two disputes in particular stood out. At Fatti's and Moni's Bellville South factory, producing flour, pasta and ice-cream cones, 78 coloured and African workers stayed out for seven months after five coloured employees were sacked because of their involvement in the Food and Canning Workers Union. The strike — the longest in South African history — ended in the re-instatement of the strikers after a national consumer boycott of Fatti's and Moni's products was organised with the support of the Soweto Committee of Ten, Inkatha yeSizwe, the Western Province African Chamber of Commerce and other community, trade-union and commercial organisations. Although won at a great price — the strike cost the union R30,000 in strike pay — the settlement was described by the Western Province General Workers Union as 'the biggest victory for workers in years'.[56] The WPGWU was itself involved in the other major dispute — a total walkout by coloured and African stevedores on 11 December 1979 forced the Cape Town dock employers to recognise a workers' committee on which the union had observers' rights (as a matter of principle the WPGWU opposed seeking recognition for itself rather than rank-and-file bodies). An attempt by the employers to use TUCSA to split the workers failed — only one person turned up at a TUCSA rally on 15 December compared with 300 at a WPGWU mass meeting called at the same time.[57] In May 1980, 18 meat factories in Cape Town went on strike after Table Bay Cold Storage had refused to recognise the WPGWU; the strike was preceded by another dispute — the workers in 11 meat firms had blacked the products of Karoo Meat Exchange, which had just victimised a worker, forcing the company to cave in. A consumer boycott of red meat was organised, leading to a 60 per cent fall in sales.

The beginning of the second schoolstudents' revolt can probably be fixed as 20 March 1980, when 600 parents and pupils attended a mass meeting in the Cape Town coloured township of Hanover Park. The grievances raised at the meeting reflected, first, the nature of coloured education. The Cape province education chief, Wouter de Vos Malan, had spelled out government policy: 'Coloured children will go into manual labour, so their education must be tailored accordingly'[58] Accordingly, per capita expenditure on school pupils in 1976-77 was: whites R654, Asians R219.96, coloureds R157.59, Africans R48.55.[59] Moreover, many schools damaged during the 1976-77 uprising had been left unrepaired. The meeting revealed great hostility towards teachers, themselves mostly coloured — one headmaster had called in the security police after he found 'SWAPO' written on a blackboard, and there were complaints about teachers' drunkenness and incompetence, as well as about compulsory fees and uniforms and the lack of student representation. Three white teachers were sacked for attending the meeting, sparking off protests by 19 schools on 5 April. Although another meeting a week later decided against a boycott, pupils at several coloured schools stayed away from class on Monday 14 April. By the end of that week 25,000 students were boycotting their schools. On 19 April the Committee of 61 (later 81 — the number of educational institutions represented) was formed. It issued a list of demands — including the right to elect student representative councils, the abolition of uniforms and corporal punishment, community involvement in education — and called a full boycott, but (with the experience of 1976-77 no doubt in mind) instructed pupils to remain at school in order to provide a framework for organisation and consciousness-raising. A hundred thousand students were estimated to be involved, including many in rural schools all over the western Cape.[60]

Several things should be noted about the boycott. First, there was the high degree of discipline and organisation displayed by the boycotters, somewhat in contrast to the rather chaotic beginnings of the 1976 uprising. Second, perhaps reflecting the longstanding influence of revolutionary socialist groups among coloureds in Cape Town, the level of political consciousness was higher than in 1976. One placard said: 'Don't force us out of school to supply cheap labour for capitalism'.[61] One worried businessman told the *Financial Times*: 'these students are arguing in terms of the class struggle, not the vague thoughts of black consciousness. That could be an ominous development.'[62] Third, although the core of the boycott was in the coloured community, it soon spread to the other oppressed groups. University students not only at the coloured University of the Western Cape, but also at Fort Hare in the eastern Cape (African) and Durban-Westville (Asian) joined in. Asian pupils in Durban boycotted classes. Although Soweto stayed comparatively quiet, dogs and tear-gas were used to disperse coloured demonstrators in Johannesburg on 18 April. African students at Mamelodi near Pretoria and Bloemfontein's Batho township (where the first fatal shooting of a demonstrator occurred) joined the boycott, which also spread to African schools in Durban and in Port Elizabeth (where pupils stoned to death a black man, armed with a knobkerrie, who was trying to get them back to school). At the beginning of June the Transkei government declared a state of emergency in response to student boycotts and demonstrations, and school unrest was reported in two other Bantustans at least — Bophuthatswana and Qwa Qwa. In July students at Morris Isaacson High School — one of the centres of the Soweto uprising in 1976 — came out in protest at the arrest of one of their number.

The regime's response was, to begin with at least, quite mild. There were no indiscriminate shootings of demonstrators, as there were in 1976, although Curtis Nkondo, an ex-president of AZAPO, was detained after attempting to address a rally in Cape Town, and some 300 protesters were detained nationally. Then, on 5 May Pieter Botha, after meeting the leaders of the coloured Cape Teachers Association, acknowledged that the students had 'justifiable grievances' and announced that he would consider a full-scale inquiry into the education system. In response, the Committee of 81 suspended the boycott, and many pupils returned to classes on 19 May. The respite was a brief one — the boycott was resumed within a few days in response to the decision by the authorities to close down Fort Hare University. On 28 May two coloured school students were shot and killed by the police at Elsies River in Cape Town. One opposition MP who visited the township was shocked by the police 'excess' he discovered — according to one report police squads attacked people walking along the pavements, provoking stone-throwing to which they retaliated with bullets.

Tensions mounted as the fourth anniversary of Soweto — 16 June — neared. On 31 May, Republic Day, troops and tanks marched through South Africa's main cities as Botha attacked protesters in a threatening speech. All public meetings on 16 June were banned and the SADF surrounded Soweto. It was in the Cape, however, that the explosion came this time. The final provocation was a 100 per cent increase in bus fares, leading to a boycott supported by coloureds and Africans alike. Calls for a national stay-at-home on 16 June were heeded mainly in Cape Town, although police fired on demonstrators in Soweto and Batho. The security forces suffered their first casualty when a white officer was stabbed to death during a baton charge near Cape Town. The day after the stay-at-home, Tuesday 17 June, the townships on the Cape Flats exploded. Young coloureds spent the afternoon building barricades out of petrol drums and burning tyres. Cars travelling along the main highway to and from David Malan airport, which passes through the Cape Flats, were stoned. The centre of the storm was at Elsies River (where Leyland South Africa has its main plant) and Retreat, but it spread as far as Paarl, in the vineyard country north-east of Cape Town, where one demonstrator was shot. Police cordons prevented journalists entering the affected areas, but it was clear that the rebels' anger led to the looting and burning of shops and vehicles owned by coloureds as well as whites, as the mass of young unemployed joined the students. The gloves came off — police commissioner General Mike Geldenhuys told his men to 'shoot to kill' (subsequently acknowledged to be 'an unfortunate choice of words' by the minister responsible, Louis Le Grange). By the morning, between 42 and 60 people had died in the cauldron on Cape Flats, and Botha's programme was in ruins.

Crackdown in Johannesburg

Although the mass movement was most advanced in the western Cape, where it involved workers, students and traders, coloureds and Africans, a series of major strikes showed that the regime was facing opposition on a nation-wide scale. Nicholas Ashford commented in *The Times* at the beginning of July that:

> in many ways the current wave of strikes ... is of greater significance for the country's future than last month's sudden outbreak of violence in the coloured townships of Cape Town ... A growing degree of labour militancy, supported by community action, ... looks like becoming a feature of South African life during the 1980s.[63]

One major dispute occurred when 7,000 workers at Frame's textile mills at Pinetown and New Germany near Durban came out on strike for a 20-25 per cent wage increase in May 1980. The Frame group was one of the firms worst hit by the mass strikes of 1973. The Durban-Pinetown area is the centre of the South African textile industry, which, although highly automated, was reliant upon a large, cheap, unskilled labour force — 70 per cent of whom were women, mostly Africans. A government-backed policy of rationalisation designed to improve the industry's weak competitive position in world markets led to a high degree of concentration, with Frame employing one-third of the textile workforce.[64] The hard-nosed pro-Nationalist management at Frame refused to recognise the FOSATU-affiliated National Union of Textile Workers and secured a ministerial order fixing wage increases at 10 per cent a year, well below the inflation rate, with the result that real wages were lower than in 1974 and half the workforce earned less than the housing subsistence level. Frame first forced the strike, then sacked all those who walked out and called in the police to arrest the strike-leaders. Workers armed with sticks battled outside the factory gates with the police, who used tear-gas to disperse them.[65] One of the strike leaders, Samson Cele, was murdered by a masked gunman in July.

The employers' response to the strikes, which paralysed the car factories at Uitenhage near Port Elizabeth for much of June and July, was quite different. At the heart of the dispute was a demand for an 80 per cent wage increase by 3,500 at the Volkswagen plant, but ten other factories — notably Goodyear — were also involved. The 7,500 strikers' bargaining position was greatly strengthened by an upturn in the car industry — sales of passenger cars rose by 22 per cent in the first half of 1980, and of commercial vehicles by 20.5 per cent, with Volkswagen taking the biggest share of the market (21 per cent).[66] The UAW was involved in the strike, persuading workers at the nearby Ford and General Motors plants in Port Elizabeth not to come out,[67] as was PEBCO, while black students in the area were among the most solid supporters of the school boycott. Ford was forced at one stage to close the Cortina assembly plant because of a shortage of components, until the parts were flown in from Britain. The police were also in evidence — they fired tear-gas and bird-shot at a mass march through central Uitenhage on 20 June and used dogs and tear-gas 'sneeze machines' to disperse 1,000 strikers who gathered outside the Goodyear plant on 25 June after they had been issued with dismissal notices by management. The Port Elizabeth-Uitenhage area was proclaimed an 'operational area', like Namibia. Protracted negotiations between the unions (UAW and NUMARWOSA) and the three main car firms led to a return to work at Volkswagen on 7 July and a wage settlement — an hourly minimum wage of R1.45, 30 cents higher than the prevailing minimum — which was only a slight improvement on the employers' initial offer of a 20 per cent increase, although they also promised to back an investigation of the workers' demand for a living wage and to discuss the introduction of a closed shop.

When the violence in the Cape was at its height white South Africa held its breath as it waited to see what would happen in Soweto. Despite a number of incidents, the township stayed quiet; even Soweto's schools were still in the state of chaos resulting from the 1976 revolt and its aftermath.[68] The passivity of Soweto arose in part from a reaction of despondency to the terrible bloodletting the township had suffered in 1976-77, in part from the political lessons drawn from that experience. Fanyana Mazibuko, secretary of the Soweto Teachers Action Committee, who was banned by the government during the new wave of unrest, explained that:

> a relatively small group of people, who have great influence because of their determination and because the guerilla struggle in Zimbabwe has given them great credibility ... are warning students not to go into the streets unarmed and provide 'cannon-fodder for the police'. That is why Soweto is quiet this time, although the rest of the country is bubbling; precisely because it tried old-fashioned protest politics and has recent experience of the way the police shot down protesters.[69]

A dramatic demonstration of the potential threat to the regime posed by armed struggle occurred on 1 June, when bombs went off at three state-owned coal-into-oil plants at Sasolburg and Secunda in the Transvaal, causing R5.8 million worth of damage. A wave of fear and rage swept white South

Africa after the explosions, for which the banned African National Congress claimed responsibility. The subsequent clampdown, involving troops surrounding the vast site at Secunda where Sasol's two new coal-into-oil plants were being built, sparked off another explosion, this time by the 18,000 black workers employed there. Infuriated by the harassment to which they were subjected — constant searches at work, confinement to their compounds after 7 p.m., omnipresent SADF patrols — the workers rioted on 14 July after one of their number, Elliot Mtetwa, was found dead in his bed — as a result, they suspected, of maltreatment by soldiers. Two huts were set alight, a bus overturned and destroyed, cars stoned and a white worker burned to death. The police were called out, and work was suspended at the site for several days. But at the beginning of August the police used tear-gas to disperse a crowd of strikers at Secunda who had attacked security guards; this time the issue was one of wages.

Meanwhile, the labour unrest had spread to Johannesburg. A brief strike by black bus drivers working for the Public Utility Transport Corporation (Putco) on 3-4 July won a 15 per cent increase, which the strikers, who were demanding over 100 per cent, accepted under protest. Then on 24 July, 650 black electricians employed by Johannesburg city control went on strike after rejecting an offer of a R4 a week increase. Apart from a substantial pay rise (they were paid R29 a week), they wanted the council to recognise the newly formed Black Municipality Workers Union (BMWU) affiliated to the Consultative Committee. By the end of July, although the electricians were drifting back to work, 10,000 black municipal workers, including most of those employed in the cleansing and engineers' departments, were out on strike backing the BMWU and demanding a R25 increase on their R33 average weekly pay. In some neighbourhoods the streets were piled up with uncollected rubbish. The city council, run by a Nationalist-dominated coalition, took a hard line, refusing to accept the opposition Progressive Federal Party's offer to act as an intermediary between them and the BMWU. They received the government's backing: after a meeting with municipal officials, Fanie Botha, the Minister of Manpower Utilisation, accused the strikers of 'bypassing the government's official conciliation machinery'.[70] Indeed this strike, like all those in 1979-80, was illegal. The city council refused to recognise the BMWU, favouring instead the parallel Union of Johannesburg Municipal Workers, which, despite the fact that it had only 40 members at the beginning of the strike, received provisional registration halfway through the dispute. Finally, on 1 August riot police descended on the municipal workers' compounds and forced 1,200 of the strikers onto buses at gunpoint. They were deported to the Bantustans — most of the municipal workers were contract labourers from the Transkei, Bophuthatswana and Venda — and Joseph Mavi, president of the BMWU, was arrested and charged with sabotage, a catch-all offence carrying a minimum penalty of five years' imprisonment and a maximum one of death. That same month the Cape meat workers strike ended in defeat after 12 weeks, also as a result of state repression.

This government strikebreaking represented the end of high hopes raised by the Wiehahn report. The *Financial Times* reported that Wiehahn himself 'is now said to be a disillusioned man whose ideas have been stifled by powerful bureaucrats'. It suggested two reasons for the authorities' response. First, the scale of the dispute — the largest involving a single employer in South African history. Second, 'industrial action has become an increasingly effective way for blacks to press for shop-floor grievances [sic] and vent political frustrations. As black workers become more organised and more militant (which they appear to be doing), the political overtones of strikes are likely to grow.'[71] However, the pattern of response was a complex one. The hard line taken by Frame and the Johannesburg council reflected the fact that in both cases the strikers were unskilled migrants or commuters. The multinationals that dominated the eastern Cape car industry adopted a different tack, confronted as they were with a much more skilled workforce. In September 1980 Ford announced that it was appointing three full-time shop stewards; Volkswagen and General Motors were expected to follow suit. Here, then, the strategy was to incorporate the independent black unions without requiring them to register under the Industrial Conciliation Act. As their role during the Ford and Volkswagen strikes suggests, the UAW and NUMARWOSA seemed quite happy to work within this framework. In November Mike Rosholt, head of the Barlow Rand investment empire, expressed his disagreement with government pleas that firms should not deal with unregistered unions.

Botha, meanwhile seemed to have reached a dead-end. The homeland leaders, notably Gatsha Buthelezi of Kwazulu, effectively killed his proposal for a separate council on which they would be represented, while coloured and Asian representatives refused to sit on the mooted President's Council unless Africans were admitted to it — a move that would cause a rebellion in the National Party. A cabinet reshuffle at the end of August 1980 strengthened the *verligtes'* hold on the government but not on the party machine. To demonstrate the regime's determination to clamp down on all opposition, black secondary schools in the Port Elizabeth-Uitenhage area were closed down in September. The blood-bath in Elsies River and the deportation of the Johannesburg strikers did not mean that Botha would make no new initiatives, but they did demonstrate the difficulties inherent in his reform programme.

Spanish capitalism had been able in the 1970s to make the transition to bourgeois democracy without seriously endangering the existing structure of economic and political power and despite the opposition of an ultra-reactionary francoist 'bunker' as obdurate as Treurnicht and the BAD bureaucracy. There, however, the regime was able to preserve the loyalty of large sections of the rural population and had the advantage that the two main workers' parties — the Communists and Socialists — were opposed to a revolutionary break with francoism. No such intermediaries between Botha and the popular masses existed in South Africa. The possible candidates for such a position — above all Chief Buthelezi, of whom more in the next chapter — would be unlikely to settle for less than a share in national political power, a demand that Botha would find difficult to concede both because of the nature of the National Party and its popular base among white workers, and the peculiar character of capital accumulation in South Africa. At the same time black workers, denied any political rights, would undoubtedly use their increasing economic power to challenge the apartheid regime. Moreover, the scope for even economic concessions was a narrow one — given the rationalisation of the labour-process, the continued reliance of South African capitalism on 'labour-repressive' export industries and the structural unemployment generated by the rising organic composition of capital. A similar problem was faced by the Brazilian regime in 1980. In response to the growing power of the working class created by the 'economic miracle' of the late 1960s and early 1970s, the Figueiredo regime initiated a gradual political 'liberalisation'. Yet when the metal-workers of Sao Paolo went on strike for the third year in succession, Figueiredo, forced by Brazil's $50 billion debt to foreign bankers to implement an austerity programme and under pressure from his own right wing, arrested the very trade-union leaders whose support was indispensable if liberalisation were not to endanger the existing order. The margin for manoeuvre is similarly narrow in South Africa. It seems unlikely that Botha will be able to buy the internal stability he is so desperately seeking.

7. Strategy and Tactics

South Africa entered the 1980s with an internally divided power bloc facing a nation-wide popular movement opposed to its rule. In this sense, it met the conditions for revolution stated in Lenin's classical definition.

> For a revolution to take place it is not enough for the exploited and oppressed masses to realise the impossibility of living in the old way, and demand changes; for a revolution to take place it is essential that the exploiters should not be able to live and rule in the old way. It is only when the *'lower classes' do not want* to live in the old way and the 'upper classes' *cannot carry on in the old way* that the revolution can triumph.[1]

This is of course too abstract. *What sort* of revolution would it be? *Which classes* would make it, and under *what leadership*? *What methods* would it use? This chapter is devoted to an attempt to answer these questions.

Class and Nation

To the first question there is a straightforward answer. South Africa is a capitalist social formation, albeit a peculiar one, in which the reproduction of the dominant relations of production requires influx control and the denial of political rights to the black majority. The disintegration of the communal relations of production which prevailed in the pre-conquest African societies has led to a situation in which the mass of the population are dependent on the sale of labour-power to white capital. In these circumstances, it is socialist revolution that is on the agenda in South Africa — not simply the introduction of black majority rule, but the expropriation of the minority of white capitalists who control the economy. This conclusion is reinforced when we consider the main thrust of the regime's strategy, spelled out by P.W. Botha as long ago as August 1976, when he told the Natal Nationalist Congress that the security of South Africa could be ensured only if 'we can succeed in establishing a strong middle class — not only among whites but among the black and brown people as well'.[2] Such a strategy has indeed been pursued in the Bantustans for many years, where the state, in collaboration with Afrikaner capital, has sought to promote the development of a collaborationist black bourgeoisie — traders, rich farmers, bureaucrats, even some small manufacturers.[3] Since Soweto this strategy has been extended to the townships, with the removal of some of the economic barriers to the development of black business, and the establishment of political institutions — the Community Councils — through which the regime hopes a privileged section of urban blacks can be persuaded to police the rest. This amounts to nothing more than what we have called the 'bantustanisation' of the townships. Its effect is likely to increase class polarisation among Africans.

At the same time, talk of the creation of a 'black labour aristocracy' among workers with section 10 rights should be treated with caution. Sheena Duncan of the liberal Black Sash suggested that, as a result of the Wiehahn and Riekert reports, section-tenners 'will now experience a considerable improvement in their everyday lives'.[4] Yet African car-workers are not being invited to join a privileged white proletariat. Indeed, the rationalisation South African capitalism is at present undergoing involves an economic offensive against white workers — they are being pushed down, while some black workers are rising a little. The minority of the African working class, whom Wiehahn and Riekert intended to benefit, are expected to become junior members of a white-dominated, state controlled, class-collaborationist trade union movement, while their wages are held down by the pressure of a massive reserve army of unemployed in the rural areas. These more skilled and better organised black workers are likely to become the vanguard of the popular resistance to the regime, not an additional prop shoring up the existing order. The strikes at Ford and Volkswagen in 1979-80 showed the willingness of these workers to fight on both economic and political fronts.

It is proletarian revolution, then, that is on the agenda in South Africa. This conclusion has been described as 'grounded not in the reality of South African life, but in the airy world of dogma'.[5] However, as this book and its predecessor *Southern Africa After Soweto* have tried to show, the existence of capitalism in South Africa is so closely bound up with that of racial oppression that it is impossible to separate the struggle against apartheid from that for socialism. It does not follow that the various forms of nationalist ideology prevailing among the black masses are, as one South African far left group believes, merely the counter-revolutionary instrument of the ruling class.[6] Capital accumulation in South Africa, because it requires the denial of political rights to the black majority, presupposes the national oppression of the African, coloured and Asian masses. It follows, first, that demands for the basic democratic freedoms — of speech, assembly, organisation, movement, universal adult suffrage — will play an essential role in popular struggles in South Africa, and, second, that the task of the revolution there will be to achieve national liberation for the oppressed majority, as well as to expropriate capital.

This means that the emergence of national consciousness is a development to be welcomed, not denounced as 'a caricature ... a dwarf ... [subject to] the will of the capitalist class'.[7] One of the great merits of the black consciousness movement has been to analyse the psychological effects of racial oppression on black people. As Steve Biko put it, describing the condition of the African community in the wake of the great defeats of the early 1960s: 'all in all the black man has become a shell, a shadow of a man, completely defeated, drowning in its own misery, a slave, an ox bearing the yoke of oppression with sheepish timidity'.[8] To rise up from this abject position, an assertion of black identity, the demand for national self-determination was a necessary and inevitable stage — a step forward on the path to revolution. To quote Lenin again:

> To imagine that social revolution is *conceivable* without revolts of small nations in the colonies and in Europe, without revolutionary outbursts by a section of the petty bourgeoisie *with all its prejudices*, without a movement of the politically non-conscious proletarian and semi-proletarian masses against oppression by the landowners, the church and the monarchy, against national oppression, etc. — to imagine all this is to *repudiate social revolution*.

> So one army lines up in one place and says, 'We are for socialism', and another, somewhere else and says, 'We are for imperialism', and that will be a social revolution! ...
> Whoever expects a 'pure' social revolution will *never* live to see it.[9]

The reality of national oppression in South Africa explains the leading role played by comparatively privileged sections of the black community in the resistance movements. An analysis of the ANC and PAC leaderships in 1957-60 revealed that 92.8 per cent of the top-rank leaders of the ANC and 73.3 per cent of those of the PAC belonged to the professional and middle classes, although a majority of lower- and middle-rank leaders were working-class.[10] The black-consciousness movement originated among African university students, a tiny and highly privileged group; the Soweto Student Representative Council, which led the 1976 uprising, was based among secondary school students, less than 15 per cent of the total African school population, and again a small and privileged minority among blacks of their age group, many of whom were unemployed 'push-outs' — 55 per cent of African pupils left school during the first four years of primary education.[11] Former schoolteachers such as Fanyana Mazibuko and Curtis Nkondo played an important role in post-uprising Soweto. Thozamile Botha was expelled from Fort Hare in 1977 and subsequently became a schoolteacher before going to work at Ford. As in Zimbabwe, sections of the African petty bourgeoisie, their advancement blocked by apartheid, adopted increasingly radical methods, placing themselves at the head of popular movements demanding a total change in the system. Despite the concessions offered to the black middle classes after Soweto, and the steady improvement in their economic position (the number of Africans in white-collar jobs was increasing rapidly), it was clear that the regime expected them to prosper only as clients of big capital and within the framework of white supremacy. Racial oppression, however, does not affect only an elite, but black people as a whole, and nationalism is therefore likely to continue to exercise enormous influence among the masses.

Considerations of this sort do not justify acceptance of the two-stage strategy advocated by the African National Congress and the South African Communist Party — first the national-democatic revolution against apartheid, then the socialist revolution against capitalism. For such a perspective presumes that national liberation can be attained in South Africa within the framework of capitalism. The interweaving of capitalist relations of production with apartheid makes this impossible. Even the bourgeois-democratic demands of universal suffrage etc. are likely to be attained only through the expropriation of the white bourgeoisie and the destruction of the state machine which defends their interests. Socialist revolution is the precondition of national liberation in South Africa, even if the development of national consciousness among the black masses provides a stimulus to the formation of class consciousness.

Resistance and Collaboration

The perspective outlined in the preceding section is rejected by the main organisations of the black resistance, all of which, whatever their other differences, agree in seeing the national liberation struggle as distinct from the class struggle. The chief difference between them lies in their conception of the *nature* of national liberation. Broadly speaking, there have been two main approaches. First, the African National Congress defined the objective of their movement as the establishment of a multiracial democratic state. This goal is outlined in some detail in the 1955 Freedom Charter, whose preamble declares that 'South Africa belongs to all who live in it, black and white.' On the other hand, the Africanists, who split from the ANC in 1959 to form the Pan Africanist Congress, took their inspiration from Anton Lembede, who wrote in 1946: 'Africa is a black man's country ... The basis of national unity is the nationalistic feeling of the Africans, the feeling of being Africans irrespective of tribal connection, social status, educational attainment or economic class'.[12]

The black consciousness movement ideologically carried on the Africanist tradition. It originated in the decision of African university students in 1969 to split away from the liberal, predominantly white NUSAS and form the all-black South African Students Organisation (SASO). Steve Biko, SASO's first president, launched a stinging attack on white liberals, whose advocacy of multiracialism, he argued, amounted to the continuation of effective white domination: 'it is rather like expecting the slave to work together with the slave-master's son to remove all the conditions of the former's enslavement.' Separate organisation in order to break down black people's 'inferiority complex' was a necessary precondition to 'true integration': 'what is necessary as a prelude to anything else is a very strong grass-roots build-up of black consciousness such that blacks can learn to assert themselves and stake their rightful claim'. The split was initially welcomed by the regime, which saw it as a step in the direction of acceptance of separate development. They soon realised their mistake when Biko attacked black leaders who participated in apartheid institutions and denounced the Bantustans as 'the greatest single fraud ever invented by white politicians'.[13]

Although influenced by contemporary developments in the United States — the black power movement and its extension, black theology (as in Zimbabwe, the various Christian churches have played an important part in shaping nationalist leaders) — as well as the writings of Frantz Fanon, the black consciousness movement (BCM) also took over two of the more politically ambiguous themes of Africanism. One was an idealisation of pre-capitalist African society as a harmonious, organic whole, free from poverty, oppression and conflict — a theme reminiscent of the rehabilitation of feudalism carried out by nostalgic conservative critics of capitalism in nineteenth century Europe. Second, the BCM rejected any analysis of contemporary South African society in terms of classes. Thus Biko dismissed white marxists who 'tell us that the situation is a class struggle rather than a racial struggle. Let them go to van Tonder in the Free State [i.e. the typical poor Afrikaner] and tell him this.' He argued that 'we should think along such lines as the "buy black" campaign once suggested in Johannesburg and establish our own banks for the benefit of the community.' The effect, combined with the tendency to see changes in terms of consciousness, the restoration of Africans' pride in their own culture and values — Biko described black consciousness as 'an inward-looking process' — led to a tendency to discount the importance of class interests embodied in, and material apparatuses underpinning, white power. In May 1976, shortly before the Soweto uprising, Biko declared that the BCM's objective was to build up black power to a point 'where whites first have to listen'. 'Our operation is basically that of bargaining', he said. 'We are not interested in armed struggle. ... We are not interested either in confrontation methods, by that meaning demonstrations which lead to definite breaking of exisiting laws, such that there is a reaction from the system.'[14]

Whatever the defects of black consciousness, SASO and the organisations it gave birth to, notably the Black People's Convention, were an essential ingredient in the black revival in the first half of the 1970s. Their message — 'Black man you are on your own!' — articulated the anger and frustration of a generation of young blacks born since the Nationalists came to power — some of them indeed after Sharpeville — whose sole experience was that of apartheid. A network of youth clubs and more openly political organisations sprang up in response to the ferment among young blacks. The most important of these was the South African Student Movement (SASM), which spread from the Soweto high schools to other parts of the country and provided the bulk of the leadership of the 1976 revolt. As one study of the uprising puts it, although 'SASM was in no sense created by SASO ... it was not born in a vacuum, and SASO was an important part of the movement of ideas and activity which engendered the climate in which black school students found their way of tackling the problems facing them.'[15] There is some controversy surrounding the subject, but there can be little doubt that the main ideological influence on the revolt was the BCM, although organisationally SASO and BPC played little part and supporters of others movements, notably the underground ANC/SACP, were also involved.[16] Equally, the BCM bore the brunt of the subsequent repression — shootings, arrests, the murder of Biko and other detainees, and the suppression on 19 October 1977 of all the organisations associated with the movement.

The resistance was not forced entirely underground, however. In May 1978 the BCM sought to regroup when the Azanian African People's Organisation (AZAPO) was launched by a meeting of 60 delegates at Roodepoort. It aimed especially to organise black workers (although much of such a plan's cutting edge was blunted by the definition of a black worker as 'any black person irrespective of professional status').[17] Although its entire executive was immediately arrested,

AZAPO was able to have some impact. A more prominent force was represented by the Soweto Committee of Ten, formed in July 1977 with the support of the Soweto Student Representative Council, Black Parents Association (BPA), SASO and the Union of Black Journalists, around the demand for a government-financed Soweto City Council in place of the puppet Community Council Pretoria was then busy installing. The committee's chairman Nthatho Motlana, a well-heeled Soweto doctor who had once been in the ANC, admitted that they were demanding 'second best':

> Soweto is part of Johannesburg and I believe that our fight should always be for direct representation on the Johannesburg city council. But I am told that the entire whites are too scared of us and our numbers.[18]

Motlana was detained for a while, and consistently rejected the regime's advances, refusing to sit on an advisory committee set up by Piet Koornhof (although he met Broederbond chairman Gerrit Viljoen) and launching in September 1979 a Soweto Civic Association in opposition to the Community Council. He hoped that an 'Afrikaner De Gaulle' (P.W. Botha?) would emerge to concede black majority rule[19] and clearly had a lot to lose in a violent upheaval. As the *Economist* put it:

> one wonders where Dr Motlana's handsome ranch bungalow and Italian car would be if the guerillas really did sweep across the Limpopo and the gates of Robben Island swung open.[20]

The principal political beneficiary of the radicalisation of black youth during and after the Soweto uprising was ensconced outside South Africa's border — the African National Congress. Many of those forced into exile joined the ANC (for example, Thozamile Botha, president of PEBCO and leader of the Ford strike). Often this was because they had no choice — an Amnesty International representative who visited Botswana in 1978 found that the police forced refugees to choose between joining the ANC or PAC or being sent back to South Africa.[21] But there were other reasons. Black consciousness, as we have seen, proved to be remarkably woolly on matters of strategy and tactics, while the ANC made no bones of its objective — the forcible overthrow of the regime — and had an armed wing, Umkonto weSizwe, which could offer military training to those who wanted to fight. Meanwhile, the PAC seemed to be disintegrating amid exile squabbles and the Unity Movement, despite continued support in the western Cape and a heroic record of struggle — notably in the peasant revolts of the 1950s and 1960s — had been forced into virtual irrelevance by the OAU's refusal to give it any backing. The BCM in exile was not immune to these problems. The ANC on the one hand denounced it — accusing Tsietsi Mashinini, an ex-president of the SSRC, of being a CIA agent — and, on the other hand sought to co-opt it claiming, for example, that 'the BPC, SASO, BPA and other similar organisations must be regarded as important tributaries to the Great River of the liberation movement headed by the ANC'.[22] The BPC found itself under pressure from the influential and rich Geneva-based International University Exchange Fund to merge with the ANC, a policy advocated by Craig Williamson, a BOSS agent who successfully infiltrated IUEF. The BCM was also internally divided, with various forces (the American and Nigerian governments in particular) pouring oil on troubled waters.

As we have already seen, the ANC sought the establishment of a multiracial democratic state. This goal was part of a strategy formulated by the South African Communist Party, the most influential political tendency within the ANC, based on a vintage stalinist stages theory, according to which the conquest of power by an alliance of the African, coloured and Asian population as a whole, plus 'white democrats' (many of the SACP leaders are white) must precede the struggle for socialism. The Communist Party central committee re-affirmed this strategy in April 1977, declaring that:

> the main content of the present phase of our struggle continues to be the national-democratic revolution to destroy internal colonialism. We believe that the achievement of this aim is in the interest not only of the black workers and peasants but also of the black petty bourgeoisie.

The rider was immediately added that 'the dominant force in this alliance must be the working class';[23] however, this formula seemed designed chiefly to justify the effective control of the ANC by the SACP, which enjoys the considerable advantage that the movement depends heavily on material support provided by the eastern bloc and Moscow's two main allies in the region, Angola and Mozambique. When a group of exiled white activists in the ANC's trade union front, SACTU, complained about the lack of serious underground work around labour issues, and called for the building of independent trade unions, they were summarily expelled.[24] Eurocommunism has yet to infect the SACP, which remains positively neanderthal in its pro-Moscow dogmatism, its journals replete with articles defending the latest twist and turn of the Kremlin's policies.[25]

The ANC/SACP's verbal radicalism was belied when it was revealed that Chief Gatsha Buthelezi, accompanied by 17 members of the Kwazulu cabinet, had met the ANC executive in London during October 1979. The two sides 'accepted each other's role and legitimacy in the struggle'.[26] To understand the significance of this move, we must take into account the peculiar place Buthelezi occupies on the South African political spectrum. As chief minister of Kwazulu he claims the leadership of five million Zulus, the largest single ethnic group in South Africa (see Table 16). His influence among the black workers in the Durban-Pinetown area is considerable: according to a survey of the members of three FOSATU unions based there, an overwhelming majority believed that African workers thought of Buthelezi as their leader.[27] The attitude taken by Buthelezi to the regime is an ambivalent one. On the one hand he denounces the apartheid system and calls for the establishment of majority rule, indeed toying with the idea of armed struggle. Thus in July 1979 he declared that 'if what I do at present in trying to bring about peaceful change is unsuccessful, I will also seriously consider crossing our borders.'[28] On the other hand, by continuing to participate in apartheid institutions, he gives the regime credibility it would otherwise lack.

Shortly before the Soweto uprising Buthelezi revived Inkatha yeSizwe, a Zulu cultural movement founded by his grandfather, King Solomon Dinuzulu, in 1928, as a national political party. By 1980 he was claiming that Inkatha had 300,000 members.[29] His hold among the Zulu of Natal was undoubtedly a major reason why Durban stayed quiet in 1976. Buthelezi smugly explained: 'Inkatha has a very strong youth-brigade and the only reason why there wasn't any, or very little, trouble in Natal was because of Inkatha'.[30] In Soweto Buthelezi's role was more pernicious. On 10 August 1976 he issued a statement calling for 'the establishment of vigilante groups to protect black property against political action' and warned 'black radicals' that they would provoke 'a backlash from the responsible elements in the black community'.[31] On 24 August during the second stay-at-home in Soweto, Zulu migrant workers living in Mzimhlope hostel, where Inkatha had a strong base, went on the rampage after being incited to do so by the police (they were actually accompanied by armoured hippos), killing at least ten people. The effect of this 'backlash' was limited: one third of the population of Soweto is Zulu, and Inkatha's appeal was limited to the most marginal section — migrant workers from rural Zululand living in appalling conditions in all-male hostels and treated with some contempt by the permanent residents. Moreover, the migrants were won over to supporting the third of the stay-at-homes, in September 1976.[32]

Table 16: African Ethnic Groups in South Africa, 1976

	('000s)
Xhosa	4,897
Zulu	5,029
Swazi	590
Sapedi	2,011
Tswana	2,103
Sheshoeshoe	1,698
Shangaan	814
Venda	449

Source: *South African Statistics, 1978*, 1.5.

Although Buthelezi denounced the police's role in inspiring the 'blacklash', young black militants not unnaturally regarded him with considerable hostility. When he tried to attend the funeral of Robert Sobukwe, founder of the PAC and one of the most revered of black leaders, on 12 March 1978 he was stoned and his bodyguards had to fire blanks into the crowd. He also had trouble inside Inkatha — in October 1978 three members of the movement's youth league were expelled for supporting 'spectacular mass action and senseless violence'.[33] His meeting with the ANC may have been motivated by the desire to increase his popular legitimacy, and at the same time to forge a united front against the black consciousness movement. Buthelezi explained in a memorandum to Richard Luce, British minister of state for foreign affairs, that 'if the future is to be stable it is vital that a central and dominating force begin to regulate black opposition to apartheid'. One of the objectives of the ANC-Inkatha alliance would be 'the elimination of ... third force factors in the black consciousness movement'.[34] ANC for its part may have hoped to gain access to potential guerilla bases in Kwazulu, and to infiltrate Inkatha. The effect of the meeting, however, could only be to strengthen Buthelezi's claim to be a genuine opponent of apartheid.

This claim was belied once again by Buthelezi's behaviour during the 1979-80 upsurge. In March 1980 in a move described by the *Financial Times* as Pretoria's 'biggest breakthrough to date in its efforts to get wider black participation in government-established institutions', Inkatha decided to stand candidates in the elections to the Community Councils, breathing life into bodies hitherto without any support.[35] (In the first elections to the Soweto Community Council, there were only 11 candidates for 30 seats and the poll in the two contested wards was 3.8 and 7.3 per cent.)[36] When school-students in Durban's Kwamashu township, administratively part of Kwazulu, joined in the national boycott in May 1980, Buthelezi clamped down brutally. *The Times* reported:

> 'Black people in Kwamashu — parents and children — were very upset with the way Chief Buthelezi forcibly dealt with the boycott', said a Kwamashu lawyer. 'He sided with the police against his own people.'
>
> The lawyer added that he knew of at least six student leaders who had subsequently been detained by the police 'at Buthelezi's behest'.[37]

Armed Inkatha supporters clashed with students at the University of Zululand when Buthelezi, the university's chancellor, attended the 1980 graduation ceremonies. The Inkatha central committee in response announced plans to introduce 'paramilitary approaches to Inkatha activity wherever possible'.[38] Shades of Muzorewa's *Pfumo reVanhu*. After the Sasol bombings Buthelezi called for the formation of black vigilante groups which would shoot to kill to protect buildings.[39] Yet he continued to be regarded as an advocate of black liberation, rather than one of its most dangerous opponents.

Armed Struggle in South Africa

The Sasol bombings brought to the attention of the world what a briefing prepared by the Anti-Apartheid Movement described as:

> one of the most significant developments in South Africa — and the least reported in the world press ... the growth of armed resistance by the national liberation movement since 1977. ... A series of skirmishes have taken place in the border regions between the freedom fighters and the South African security forces. There have been many armed attacks against police stations, security police and informers in South Africa. South African police have announced the discovery of tens of thousands of arms caches at widely separated locations, indicating that the movement has succeeded in infiltrating large numbers of freedom fighters and considerable numbers of arms.[40]

This offensive was largely, although not wholly, the work of the ANC's armed wing, Umkonto weSizwe, which was able to establish itself not only in some of the front-line states — Angola, Botswana and Mozambique, but also in Lesotho and Swaziland, statelets surrounded on all sides by South Africa (although Swaziland has a common border with Mozambique, which makes it a particularly attractive means of access to northern Natal and eastern Transvaal). The ranks of the guerillas were swelled by the 'graduates' — young blacks forced to flee South Africa after the uprising, many of whom joined the ANC. Brigadier C.F. Zietsman, head of the security police, estimated in June 1978 that there were 4,000 black South Africans undergoing military training in different parts of Africa.[41] Compared with the haphazard and disastrous sabotage campaign organised by the ANC in the early 1960s, the new offensive was a model of professionalism. A bombing campaign in 1977 gave way to a series of armed actions. Some of the major incidents are listed in Table 17.

Table 17: Armed struggle in South Africa, 1976-80

October 1976	Bomb explosion in Jabulani police station, Soweto
30 November 1976	Four ANC fighters arrested on Swaziland/Mozambique border but escape
13 June 1977	Gun battle in Gooch St, Johannesburg, between two armed blacks and police
9 September 1977	Sergeant Leonard Nkósi, security police detective and ex-ANC member, assassinated in Kwamashu, Durban
26 September 1977	ANC guerillas killed and two SAP wounded in gun battle near Dobsonville
2 November 1977	One guerilla killed, another captured after gun battle near northern Natal border with Swaziland
4 November 1977	Bomb explodes at Carlton Centre, Johannesburg, injuring 17 people
6 December 1977	Bomb explodes at police station near Johannesburg
13 December 1977	Policeman shot and killed near Grahamstown
8 January 1978	Police informer shot and wounded in Kwamashu
19 January 1978	Hand grenade thrown into the house of police informer in Alexandra, Johannesburg
February 1978	SAP patrol ambushed near Swaziland border
3 March 1978	White farmer shot dead near Botswana border
26 June 1978	Senior black detective, Sergeant Orphan Chapi, shot dead in Soweto
July 1978	Black BOSS agent shot dead in Umlazi, Durban
August 1978	Engagement between Umkonto and SADF/SAP/Bophuthatswana National Guard in eastern Transvaal. ANC claims ten 'racist soldiers' killed
25 September 1978	Nicholas Molokwani, Soweto teacher, shot dead by SAP, who claim he is ANC 'terrorist'
27 October 1978	Two 'terrorists' killed in Bophuthatswana
30 October 1978	SAP sergeant wounded in gun battle with guerillas between Louis Trichardt and Botswana border

19 November 1978	Jimmy Kruger, Minister of Justice, Police and Prisons claims that group of PAC 'terrorists' recently entered South Africa
13 January 1979	SAP intercept ANC guerillas near Botswana border, killing one and capturing another
29 January 1979	BOSS agent shot dead in Umlazi
24 February 1979	Security police confirm capture of two 'terrorists' in eastern Transvaal
21 March 1979	Security policeman shot in Sebokeng, Vereeniging
1 May 1979	Three ANC fighters attack Moroka police station, Soweto, with AK-47 rifles and hand grenades and escape after killing one constable
28 June 1979	Johannesburg Ramagacha, ex-police sergeant arrested in connection with 1 May attack, escapes from Protea police station, killing one policeman and wounding five others
2 November 1979	Orlando police station, Soweto, attacked by at least four men armed with AK-47s and hand grenades, two constables killed
4 January 1980	Three armed men attacked Soekmekaar police station in northern Transvaal
26 January 1980	Three ANC guerillas hold 25 hostages at bank in Silverton, Pretoria, demanding release of Nelson Mandela and other political prisoners. SAP shoot and kill them and one hostage
19 February 1980	SAP disclose that guerillas attacked store in Pelindaba, 40 km. from Mozambique border, and that they have discovered huge armed caches in the area — 'enough to start a small war'
21 February 1980	The SADF announce that they have taken over control of northern Natal from the SAP
4 March 1980	Booysens police station, in a white suburb of Johannesburg, attacked with rockets, grenades and guns
1 June 1980	The ANC sets off bombs at Sasol One and Natref plants at Sasolburg, near Vereeniging, and Sasol Two at Secunda

Source: Anti-Apartheid Movement, *The Battle for South Africa*

The degree of popular support for this campaign can be gauged by the reaction in Soweto to the Silverton bank siege. The ANC guerillas involved in the siege came from the township and had left the country after 1976. They were buried in Soweto. Two thousand people attended the funeral of William Madela on 6 February 1980. They sang freedom songs, made black power salutes and chanted '*Amandla*!' ('Power!') and 'He was not a terrorist, he was a hero.' Police used tear-gas to disperse the crowd; they did so again three days later, when 5,000 mourners paid tribute to Fannie Mafoko. A poll revealed that three-quarters of Sowetans sympathised with the three young men killed by the police.[42] Nor was the armed struggle confined to the cities, as Table 17 shows. *US News and World Report*'s Pretoria correspondent wrote in March 1980:

> Some rural areas already resemble battle zones, just as did regions in neighbouring Rhodesia at the height of the country's civil war.
>
> Schools in the Middleburg area, 100 miles east of Johannesburg, have been issued sandbags. In northern Natal province, close to the border of Mozambique, farmers carry weapons wherever they go and keep in contact with each other by radio. Police stations in the isolated frontiers with Botswana have been attacked, and many farms in the region have been deserted by whites fearful of guerilla raids.[43]

Indeed it is the countryside that, in the long term, the most serious military threat to the regime is likely to arise. This especially so because of the importance of the Bantustans both in providing an avenue for at least some black political aspirations and in serving as the institutional framework through which the reserve army of unemployed workers is regulated and controlled. The homelands are an economic disaster area — their average national income per capita rose from R101 to R253 in 1970-75 — but only R32 and R73 respectively was generated from within the Bantustans, the rest deriving mainly from migrants' remittances. The eight per cent real growth in GDP clocked up in the Bantustans annually between 1970 and 1975 was mainly the result of increased government spending,[44] much of it financed by Pretoria, which supplied in 1978-79 R293.5 million to the homeland governments and R147.3

million to the 'independent' states of the Transkei and Bophuthatswana.[45] When Venda became 'independent' in September 1979 migrants made up over 70 per cent of national income, while five-sixths of its budget came from South African subsidies.[46] The three 'independent' Bantustans were known as the 'casino states' because one of their few growth industries was the provision of services prohibited in the rest of South Africa such as gambling and multiracial sex to holidaying whites. Agricultural production was largely the monopoly of a handful of landowners and rich peasants (some eight per cent of rural households in the Transkei).[47] The Wiehahn and Riekert reports, involving as they did a strategy of dividing the section-tenners, with the right to reside in urban areas, from the mass of unemployed and migrants, was likely to fuel discontent in the homelands. The *Financial Mail* suggested that:

> the real problem for the government is likely to come from the rural areas ...
>
> Huge pools of unemployed, resentful people in the Bantustans, who see themselves now formally excluded from the new system, are likely to be fertile recruiting grounds for the insurgents.[48]

There were signs that the South African military were becoming increasingly worried about the Bantustans. The *Economist* commented:

> One has only to look at a map of homeland South Africa to see why. The proliferation throughout 'white' South Africa of black-controlled refuges to add to the existing scatter of Botswana, Lesotho, Swaziland and the Transkei would present a near-impossible policing, however compliant the black homeland defence forces might be. The new 'state' of Bophuthatswana includes territory just half an hour's drive from the centre of Pretoria. and the contiguous Transkei, Ciskei, Kwazulu territories on the eastern seaboard, packed with dispossessed black Africans, are not ideal neighbours for a nervous white government.[49]

Kwazulu presents a particularly acute problem, since it consists of 48 fragments running from the border with Mozambique and Swaziland through the white-owned sugar plantations of northern Natal to the townships of Durban. It does not require much imagination to foresee, should Buthelezi's popular base be undermined, the whole apparatus of people's war springing up in Kwazulu, guerillas, liberated areas, *mujibas* and all.

There are some indications of the seriousness with which the SADF now considers the problem. Botha's generals are not fools. 'They have read their Vietnam manuals. They have studied French experience in Algeria and British performance in Ulster and taken a front seat in Rhodesia.'[50] Understanding that, in the words of one counter-insurgency expert, 'an insurgent movement is a war for the people',[51] they have made some efforts to win the 'hearts and minds' of Afrcans (indeed, it is this essentially military assessment of the situation that provides much of the thrust behind Botha's reform programme). It was announced in August 1979 that for the previous 18 months SADF Natal Command's Civil Action Programme had 58 personnel in Kwazulu working as doctors, agricultural advisers etc.[52]

The SADF might well have sympathised with the growing opposition to the planned consolidation of the Bantustans into more compact and economically viable areas. Buying out white farmers in areas marked for inclusion in the homelands would remove an important advance guard in the battle against guerilla incursions. (In a separate move to combat the white depopulation of certain militarily important rural areas, the government announced in May 1979 that it would provide soft loans for farmers with military training to settle in the cattle-ranching areas of the northern Transvaal within 50 km. of the border and in the vegetable farming area of Komatipoort within 30 km. of the Mozambique border.)[53]

At the beginning of August 1980 Professor Jan Lombard, one of Botha's advisers, dropped a bombshell when he proposed scrapping consolidation and instead creating a confederation of eight regions. In Natal he proposed a multiracial government representing three zones — the white rural areas, the Durban-Pinetown metropolis and Kwazulu. The Lombard report was commissioned by the Natal sugar producers, who believed that the proposed consolidation of Kwazulu into ten areas would lead to a drastic fall in cane production and the closure of some sugar mills. Sugar accounts for some 60 per cent of the province's agricultural output[54] and 'is for Natal what gold is for South Africa', according to the chairman of the South African Sugar Association.[55] Lombard's proposal to create a multiracial 'KwaNatal' was supported by Buthelezi and the opposition Progressive Federal Party but rejected by the Natal Nationalists.

The interlocking military and economic considerations involved in the debate about consolidation reflect with precision the thinking behind Botha's reform programme. The national strategic planners grouped around the State Security Council in Pretoria are preparing for a major guerilla war in the South African countryside. Part of their preparations involves the creation of armed forces in the Bantustans — the Bophuthatswana and Venda National Guards are of particular importance because of these 'states' location in sensitive border areas. A SADF brigadier has been seconded to the former force, while an ex-security policeman commands the latter. The escalation of fighting in northern Natal (responsibility for whose security was assumed by the SADF in February 1980) would almost certainly see the use of the increasingly paramilitary Inkatha to provide an auxiliary force to the regime's troops.

Does this mean that liberation will come in South Africa as it did in Zimbabwe — through people's war in the countryside? The answer is almost certainly no. My reason for saying this is not that rural struggles are somehow irrelevant to the South African situaion. On the contrary, although the mass of the population has been proletarianised, the function performed by the Bantustans as a dumping ground for the unemployed means that a significant portion of the South African working class, the reserve army of labour, is bottled up in them, and that they will therefore inevitably be, as they were from the 1930s to the 1960s, important centres of resistance to the regime. The exclusion of Africans from the bulk of the land is a structural feature of South African capitalism and is likely to remain a potent source of popular grievance and mass struggle.

There are more general difficulties with a guerilla strategy in South Africa, whether its focus is in the countryside or in the towns (where, as Table 17 shows, much of the fighting since 1976 has occurred). There is hardly any example of a guerilla war leading to the physical defeat of the enemy forces: in almost every case of victory by the insurgents, it was won in a colonial situation where, by conducting a war of attrition, they succeeded in undermining the will of the metropolitan power to fight. One of the few possible exceptions is the first Indochina war, against the French — certainly final victory was won in Vietnam in 1975 only after the US had effectively withdrawn its support for the Saigon regime and by means of a conventional military offensive employing armour, artillery etc. The record of successful *urban* guerilla struggles is even more scant — the FLN won in Algeria *despite* their defeat in the Battle of Algiers. The South African regime does not depend for its existence on any colonial power. It represents capitalist interests which are heavily dependent on the white monopoly of political power. It is armed to the teeth, has plentiful experience of counter-insurgency operations (both in Namibia and Zimbabwe and, inside South Africa, during the revolts in the Reserves between the late 1930s and early 1960s) and has been preparing for armed confrontation within its borders for many years. Those who expect guerilla struggle as such to bring down the apartheid regime have a long wait ahead of them.

Furthermore, there is a danger that concentration exclusively on the organisation of armed struggle will lead to the creation of a guerilla army which operates as a military elite alienated from the mass of the population. Mass struggles would be seen in such a case as playing merely an instrumental and supportive role. The existence of such an attitude is evident in a recent article on armed struggle in the SACP journal. The author denies that:

> a revolutionary situation [in Lenin's sense] is always a prerequisite of the armed struggle ... Experience of other countries like Algeria, Cuba, Angola, on the contrary, shows that guerilla struggle can bring about a revolutionary situation ... As in Algeria, Cuba and other places, the general uprising will be sparked off by organised and well equipped guerilla operations during the course of which the masses of the people will be drawn in and armed.[56]

Apart from a rather eccentric approach to historical fact (in neither Algeria nor Angola was colonialism destroyed by a 'general uprising' but by the domestic political and economic crises unleashed within the metropolitan power by the war of liberation, while the comparison of the Botha regime with the latter days of Batista in Cuba is just a joke) the article, and the strategy it advocates, clearly consider armed struggle as a matter of spectacular armed actions against the forces of the state — such as the numerous attacks mounted by the ANC on police stations. Despite the heroism and efficiency with which these actions have been mounted, a strategy based upon them is unlikely to be unsuccessful. In the first place, as the victory of the French during the Battle of Algiers, and the successful counter-insurgency operations mounted by the military in Brazil, Uruguay and Argentina during the 1970s show, urban guerilla offensive of this sort can be repelled, provided that the regime is prepared to be sufficiently ruthless and has the necessary resources, manpower and intelligence available. Second, it is quite false that, as the SACP writer argues, 'in terms of political mobilisation of the masses, such MK [Umkonto we Sizwe] operations as the Soweto Police Assaults are ideal operations.' Undoubtedly they won the support and admiration of the Soweto people — but did they mobilise them? Of necessity such operations require secrecy, a cell-structure, etc, — methods which by their very nature prevent mass involvement in them. The masses become spectators, looking on while the heroic Umkonto weSizwe fighters battle the police. The effects of such a strategy on mass work are suggested by one of the documents produced by the group expelled from SACTU, which attacked the tendency [within the ANC] ... which holds that SACTU's role is to serve as a "signpost", directing workers to Umkonto weSizwe ... a mere agency for the recruitment of individuals for guerilla training'.[57] Given the objective significance of the black labour movement in the struggle against apartheid, such an approach could only be disastrous in its consequences.

None of this should be taken to imply a rejection of armed struggle as such. In the first place, there is no doubt that apartheid can only be removed by armed insurrection and the physical destruction of the existing state apparatus. However, the success or failure of such an uprising will depend upon the mobilisation of the black masses. Apartheid, like capitalism generally, has created its own gravediggers — the African working class upon whose labour the wealth and might of white South Africa depends. The basis for effective armed struggle can only be laid by developing the collective organisation and self-confidence of the black working class through struggles which are in the first instance economic. Second, guerilla struggle in the countryside, even if it cannot deliver the deathblow to the regime, is of great importance. It is the only means through which a very significant section of the black working class — the unemployed and partially employed in the Bantustans — can be drawn into struggle against the regime. This implies a certain sort of guerilla strategy — that pursued by ZANU-PF in Zimbabwe, which involved both undermining the structure of rural administration and drawing the mass of the population into an alternative political framework, rather than the narrower militarism of the ANC. (Of course, there are many problems involved in such an approach — the African rural economy is much weaker than in Zimbabwe, and, as we saw, ZANU-PF used the popular mobilisation in the liberated areas to lay the basis for a monolithic party.) There is a tradition of such struggles in the South African countryside. Rural guerilla warfare could undoubtedly debilitate the regime, by forcing Pretoria to divert more and more resources into policing the black population. Already the Namibian war, and the growing casualties it is causing the SADF, is fuelling opposition to conscription among young whites. As the war spreads inside South Africa itself, the regime's vulnerability will grow. What Marx wrote in 1856 of the country where the 'labour-repressive' 'Prussian' mode of capitalist development originated is equally applicable to South Africa: 'The whole thing in Germany will depend on the possibility of backing the proletarian revolution by some second edition of the Peasant War. Then the affair will be splendid.'[58]

Party and Class

Implicit in the perspective argued for here is an awareness of the importance of the black trade unions. For it is through the confidence and organisation developed out of successful economic struggles — over wages, conditions etc. — that black workers can acquire the consciousness and strength necessary to take on the regime. A variety of important questions are posed by strategy centred on the black labour movement, which we shall try to touch on in this concluding section. First, we have talked about the *black* working class. The notion that the way forward lies through uniting black and white workers is a dangerous delusion. The objective basis for workers' unity lies in their shared relation to the means of production — their separation from them and the consequent compulsion to sell their labour-power to capital. Now while white workers are still workers in this basic sense, they have been able to build up such a vast collection of privileges, deriving ultimately from their representation in the state and blacks' exclusion, and from white capital's strategy of dividing workers along racial lines, that they are alienated from the mass of the South African proletariat. It is true that white workers' economic privileges are now under attack. However, the effect of this attack is to drive them *rightwards*, to assert with increasing desperation their membership of the superior race. It may be that in time to come some white workers will throw in their lot with their black brothers and sisters. Until that happens, the priority will remain the development of the black workers' movement.

The most important issue raised by the 1979-80 disturbances was that of the relation between trade-union and political struggles. FOSATU adopted a 'no politics' approach, concentrating on questions of trade-union organisation and recognition, while at Ford Thozamile Botha and the PEBCO activists insisted that the struggle against white supremacy took priority over all other issues. This was a false polarity. The interlocking system of racial oppression and class exploitation in South Africa meant that economic and political struggles could not be neatly separated. At the same time the experience of the 1950s suggested that an exclusively political approach contained dangers — SACTU, as part of the Congress Alliance, had then concentrated on the political campaigns initiated by the ANC to the detriment of economic issues (the depressed economic climate of the 1950s made it difficult to win trade-union battles in any case). Economic struggles provide an indispensable training ground, giving workers a sense of their collective strength and selecting the leadership for the wider political confrontations. To make trade unions essentially political organisations, as those expelled from SACTU argued when they called for 'an independent revolutionary trade union organisation',[59] would not only invite immediate suppression by the state, it would prevent trade unions from fulfilling their most elementary functions as organisations fighting to improve workers' conditions within the framework of capitalism and open to all who qualified for membership in terms of their job irrespective of their political views. It is probable that the prevailing ideology among the mass of black workers in South Africa is a mixture of nationalism and tribalism; these ideas will be replaced by revolutionary socialist ones only through the experience of struggle, and in the main of trade union struggles.

Yet unless the independent unions are committed to the improvement of the condition of the black working class *as a whole*, migrants and section-tenners alike, and, as its necessary condition, the introduction of democratic rights for the oppressed majority, they will be vulnerable to the strategy of incorporation pursued by the more sophisticated wing of South African capital — notably the car multinationals. The conduct of the UAW and NUMARWOSA during the Ford and Volkswagen strikes shows that the 'no politics' approach can lead to the leaders of the independent unions acting as policemen whose aim is to defuse the struggle rather than develop it. UAW organiser George Manaase said after the Ford strike: 'political organisations coming to interfere with us — these militant radicals, that is our major obstacle'.[60] Thozamile Botha said of FOSATU: 'They do not want to confront management. They want to solve things by peaceful means ... They don't want to confront or to organise for strikes ... They always persuade the workers to go back to work'.[61] Recognition would be a poor gain if bought at the price of creating a black trade union bureaucracy. Of course, the tendency towards the emergence of a layer of full-time officials alienated from the shop floor and concerned to negotiate class compromise rather than wage class struggle is inherent in trade unionism, and is reinforced in South Africa by the highly bureaucratic and collaborationist nature of the mainstream unions. The problem is to find ways of combating this tendency. This is an issue of far greater importance than the purely tactical one of whether or not to register under the Industrial Conciliation Act, where FOSATU may quite well be right in seeking registration.

These conflicts — between politics and economics, workplace and community, town and country — would depend for their resolution on the emergence of a revolutionary party capable of acting as, in Lenin's words:

> *the tribune of the people*, who is able to react to every manifestation of tyranny and oppression, no matter where it appears, no matter what stratum or class of the people it affects; who is able to generalise all these manifestations and produce a single picture of police violence and capitalist exploitation; who is able to take advantage of every event, however small, in order to set forth *before all* his socialist convictions and his democratic convictions, in order to clarify for *all* and everyone the world-historic significance of the struggle for the emancipation of the proletariat.[62]

The largely spontaneous and unco-ordinated character of the struggles in the 1970s — Durban blew up in 1973, but stayed quiet in 1976, while in 1980 Soweto took the back seat when strikes and boycotts shook the rest of the country — has to some degree been a source of strength, since the regime could not cut off the movement's head by arresting its leaders. Centralised political leadership will, however, be essential in the 1980s, when the problem will be one of co-ordinating and directing different struggles as part of a nation-wide movement capable, in the appropriate conditions, of wresting power from the white minority. Centralised leadership alone would not suffice: avoidance of the monolithic one-party model found in Angola and Mozambique would depend on whether mass struggles led to the formation of organs of popular power within which the revolutionary party fought for support rather than imposing its will.

Such a party, formed through a genuine interaction between leadership and masses, would require great clarity about the working-class character of South African revolution and its socialist objectives, combined with considerable tactical flexibility, the willingness to use a variety of methods in the struggle against apartheid. It could develop only if sections of the black resistance were prepared to embrace revolutionary socialism and to involve themselves in the struggles in the factories and mines where the power to destroy apartheid lay.

There is a final corollary to our analysis. South African society contains in microcosm the structure of world capitalism

— a tiny, highly centralised ruling class perched atop a proletariat that is itself deeply divided between a comparatively privileged white minority, the mass of semi-skilled and unskilled manual workers and, at the bottom, the unemployed and underemployed in their rural misery. Racial oppression in its different forms, including P.W. Botha's 'neo-apartheid', arose from the dynamic of capital accumulation in South Africa, itself a subordinate part of the world economy whose structure it mirrors. That international system was able in 1980 to force ZANU-PF, one of the most radical movements to have taken power in the third world, to bow down before its laws. Even 'People's' China and 'socialist' Poland are increasingly drawn into its rhythms.

Yet world capitalism is in crisis. It entered the 1980s in recession, and with its control over parts of the third world faltering, above all in the Middle East in the wake of the Iranian revolution. Poland and Brazil as well as South Africa experienced major outbursts of working-class struggle in 1980. The explosions were in each case the product of a contradictory process of development, in which dependent capitalist formations, irrespective of their rulers' political complexions, sought to achieve autarky through large-scale state investments. This solution paradoxically bound them closer to the world economy, because it led them to import capital goods from the advanced capitalist countries which could only be financed by exports or loans from western banks. It also created in each of these countries a powerful industrial working class no longer willing to accept low wages and state repression. The hope that weaker economies such as Zimbabwe could succeed where Poland or Brazil had failed was a feeble one. All were part of a world system whose dynamic was transmitted by the fluctuations of the international market, as South Africa learned to its cost in the mid-1970s. Only an international revolution, based on the unity of workers in different countries against both their own rulers and the multinationals, could end the system so well epitomised by apartheid South Africa.

References

For abbreviations used see page 180

Introduction 1-7

1. J. Acton, 'Paper hats and half-price books', *NS*, 25 April 1980.
2. Interview in *Africa*, No. 104, April 1980.
3. *Zimbabwe News*, July-August 1979.
4. *FM*, 11 January and 7 March 1980.
5. *Observer*, 6 July 1980.
6. *Times*, 25 July 1980.
7. Quoted in M. Meredith, *The Past is Another Country*, London: Andre Deutsch, 1979, p. 212.
8. *Sunday Telegraph*, 21 April 1980.
9. *Now!*, 18-24 April 1980.
10. *Guardian*, 29 May 1980.
11. Peter Yonghusband in *Daily Mail*, 19 June 1980.
12. *Times*, 19 June 1980.
13. A. Callinicos and J. Rogers, *Southern Africa after Soweto*, London: Pluto, 1977, p. 9.

1. A Region in Crisis 8-23

1. Although R.W. Johnson thinks otherwise. His *How Long Will South Africa Survive?*, London: Macmillan, 1977, is far and away the best guide to the diplomatic manoeuvrings in and around southern Africa in the first two-thirds of the 1970s. Unfortunately, those fighting white power figure only as abstractions or as the butts of the author's witticisms.
2. R. Blake, *A History of Rhodesia*, London: Eyre Methuen, 1977, p. 343.
3. See G. Arrighi, 'The political economy of Rhodesia', in G. Arrighi and J. Saul, *Essays in the Political Economy of Africa*, London and New York: Monthly Review Press, 1973.
4. Blake, *op. cit.* p. 384.
5. See A. Callinicos and J. Rogers, *Southern Africa after Soweto*, London: Pluto, 1977, pp 69-78. See also chapter six above.
6. See *ibid.* chapter five.
7. See chapter two above for a sketch of African nationalism in Zimbabwe.
8. See *Guardian*, 16 February 1976.
9. See R. Hallett, 'The South African intervention in Angola 1975-76', *African Affairs*, vol. 77 no. 308, July 1978; Callinicos and Rogers, chapter seven; Johnson, chapter eight; and J. Stockwell, *In Search of Enemies*, London: Futura, 1979.
10. *Observer*, 7 March 1976.
11. See *The Kissinger Study of Southern Africa*, Nottingham: Spokesman Books, 1976.
12. Quoted in F. Richards, 'The new scramble for Africa', *Revolutionary Communist Papers*, no. 5, September 1979.

13. S. Clarke, *Changing Patterns of International Investment in South Africa and the Disinvestment Campaign*, London: Anti-Apartheid Movement, 1978, table 2 (ii) p. 26; and A. Spandau, *Economic Boycott against South Africa*, Kenwyn: Juta & Co, 1979, p. 116.
14. Quoted in C. Legum and T. Hodges, *After Angola*, London: Rex Collings, 1976, p. 27.
15. *Times*, 10 December 1976.
16. R.W. Johnson believes, rather implausibly, that Kissinger compelled Vorster to accede to the deal by forcing down the gold price and cutting off loans to South Africa (see Johnson, *op. cit* chapter ten). See chapter six above for a discussion of movements in the gold price.
17. *FT*, 1 November 1976.
18. M. Meredith, *The Past is Another Country*, London: Andre Deutsch, 1979, p. 242.
19. On the Kissinger mission and its aftermath, see Callinicos and Rogers, *op. cit.* chapter nine; Johnson, *op. cit.* chapters ten and eleven; and Meredith, *op. cit.* pp. 242-66.
20. Z. Brzezinski, 'America in a hostile world', *Foreign Policy*, no. 23, Summer 1976, pp. 70, 73, 95.
21. *FM*, 30 September 1977.
22. *South African Reserve Bank Bulletin*, March 1980.
23. *FM*, 10 August 1979.
24. *FT*, 24 July 1980.
25. Quoted in B. Cohen, *The Black and White Minstrel Show* (Nottingham: Spokesman Books, 1977) p. 8.
26. Brzezinski, p. 96.
27. *FM*, 27 May 1977.
28. *Newsweek*, 29 September 1980.
29. G. Cox, 'Western strategy in southern Africa', in Western Massachusetts Association of Concerned African Scholars (eds.), *US Military Involvement in Southern Africa*, Boston: South End Press, 1978, p. 52.
30. *Economist*, 14 May 1977.
31. See J.Ph. Peemans, 'The social and economic development of Zaire since independence', *African Affairs*, 74:295, April 1975; and A. Harding, 'The rape of Zaire', *Revolutionary Communist Papers*, no 5, September 1979.
32. *Economist*, 25 December 1976.
33. See G. Hull, 'The French connection in Africa: Zaire and South Africa', *Journal of Southern African Studies*, 5:2, April 1979; and B. Patel, 'France and the fall of Bokassa', *Socialist Review*, no. 16, November/December 1979.
34. *Newsweek*, 29 September 1980. See also *Resister* no 10, Sept/Oct 1980. For a sceptical view of South Africa's importance to the west, see W. Foltz, 'US policy towards southern Africa: economic and strategic constraints', in R Lemarchand (ed.), *American Policy in Southern Africa*, Washington: University of America Press, 1978.

2. The rise of Robert Mugabe 24-51

1. See T.O. Ranger, *Revolt in Southern Rhodesia, 1896-7*, London: Heinemann, 1967.
2. *Economic Survey of Rhodesia, 1977*, table 10, p. 19.
3. The source of these figures is R. Riddell, *The Land Question in Rhodesia*, Gwelo: Mambo Press, 1978.
4. P.S. Harris, *Black Industrial Workers in Rhodesia*, Gwelo: Mambo Press, 1974, p. 9.
5. *Ibid.* p. 29.

6. See D.G. Clarke, *Agricultural and Plantation Workers in Rhodesia*, Gwelo: Mambo Press, 1977.
7. The best account of this period is N. Shamuyarira, *Crisis in Rhodesia*, London: Andre Deutsch, 1965. For a vivid personal memoir see L. Vambe, *From Rhodesia to Zimbabwe*, London: Heinemann, 1976.
8. One account of the armed struggle in the 1960s and the subsequent splits is K. Maxey, *The Fight for Zimbabwe*, London: Rex Collings, 1975, chapters two and five. See also R. Gibson, *African Liberation Movements*, London: Oxford University Press, 1972, part four.
9. See A.K. Weinrich, *Black and White Elites in Rural Rhodesia*, Manchester: Manchester University Press, 1973.
10. See *Report of the Commission on Rhodesian Opinion*, Cmnd. 4964, London: HMSO, 1972; and J. Todd, *The Right to Say No*, London: Sidgwick and Jackson, 1972.
11. See Maxey, *op. cit.* chapter six; and A. Wilkinson, 'From Rhodesia to Zimbabwe', in B. Davidson, J. Slovo, A. Wilkinson, *Southern Africa: The New Politics of Revolution*, Harmondsworth: Penguin, 1976.
12. Our account of the role of the ZANU old guard closely follows that in T.O. Ranger, 'Politicians and soldiers: The re-emergence of the Zimbabwe African National Union', Conference on Zimbabwe, Leeds University, 21-22 June 1980.
13. Quoted, *ibid.* p. 7.
14. Quoted, *ibid.* p. 6.
15. *Observer*, 30 December 1979. This supports the version of events given in A. Callinicos and J. Rogers, *Southern Africa after Soweto*, London: Pluto, 1977, pp. 125-31.
16. See Callinicos and Rogers, *op. cit.* chapter nine.
17. See Vambe, *op. cit.* pp. 81-90, for a description of Kutama where 'young Africa, full of hope and zeal' came to study.
18. Ranger, *op. cit.* pp. 7-9.
19. Memorandum by ANC fighters at Mgagao Military Camp in Tanzania.
20. *Africa Confidential*, 3 December 1976.
21. Tongogara and the other *Dare* members had kept in touch with the ZANU leadership through Simon Muzenda, Simbi Mubako and others. See D. Mitchell, *African Nationalist Leaders in Zimbabwe: Who's Who 1980*, Salisbury: D. Mitchell, 1980, pp. 18-19, 32-3.
22. A.K.H. Weinrich, 'Strategic resettlement in Rhodesia', *JSAS* 3:2 April 1977.
23. *Africa Confidential*, 9 May 1975.
24. *Zimbabwe News*, July-August 1979.
25. *Ibid.*
26. Interview with Alex Callinicos, 26 February 1980.
27. *FT*, 'Survey on Zimbabwe', 22 April 1980.
28. R. Riddell, 'Education for employment', *From Rhodesia to Zimbabwe* no. 8, London: CIIR, 1980, p. 80.
29. *Africa Confidential*, 25 April 1979.
30. L. Cliffe and B. Munslow, 'The 1980 Zimbabwe elections: how they were won and what they mean', Conference on Zimbabwe, Leeds University, 21-22 June 1980.
31. *Ibid.*
32. *Ibid.*
33. B.H. Masanu, 'The Zimbabwe independence elections in Mashonaland Central Province', Conference on Zimbabwe, Leeds University, 21-22 June 1980, p. 8.
34. See M. Bourdillon, *The Shona Peoples*, Gwelo: Mambo Press, 1976, chapters 8, 9, 10.
35. J.M.M. Mpofu, 'The February 1980 Zimbabwe elections: the Matabeleland North and South Provinces', Conference on Zimbabwe, Leeds University, 21-22 June 1980.

36. *Africa Confidential*, 24 June 1977.
37. M. Meredith, *The Past is Another Country*, London: Andre Deutsch, 1979, pp. 302-4.
38. Quoted *ibid*. p. 292.
39. Johannesburg *Star* International Airmail Weekly, 6 August 1977.
40. See *Rhodesia's Internal Settlement*, London: Catholic Institute for International Relations, 1978; and *Smith's Settlement*, London: International Defence and Aid Fund, 1978.
41. *RH*, 23 March 1978.
42. *Herald*, 15 August 1978.
43. *RH*, 6 March 1978.
44. *Ibid*. 14 April 1978.
45. *Sunday Mail*, 27 August 1978.
46. Meredith, *op. cit*. p. 351.
47. See *ibid*. pp. 345-8; and *Economist*, 9 September 1978.
48. *Africa Confidential*, 9 June 1978.
49. See *Free and Fair? The 1979 Rhodesia Election*, a report by observers on behalf of the British Parliamentary Human Rights Group.
50. *Africa Confidential*, 20 June 1979.
51. *Herald*, 15 August 1978.
52. *Africa Confidential*, 25 April 1979.
53. 'War review', *Zimbabwe News*, July-August 1979.
54. *FM*, 5 January 1979.
55. *Times*, 20 June 1980.
56. *FT*, 22 August 1980.
57. *Guardian*, 'Special Report on Nigeria', 11 August 1980.
58. See H. Stephenson, *Mrs Thatcher's First Year*, London: Jill Norman, 1980, pp. 78-88.
59. *FT*, 'Survey on Zimbabwe', 22 April 1979.
60. R. Riddell, 'Alternative development strategies for Zimbabwe', 'Issues in development' seminar, Centre for Interracial Studies, University of Rhodesia, 18 February 1980, p. 4.
61. P. Moorcraft, *A Short Thousand Years*, Salisbury: Galaxie Press, 1980, p. 187.
62. Riddell, *op. cit*. p. 4.
63. *The Constitution of Zimbabwe*, Salisbury: the Government Printer, 1979, p. 16.
64. *New Statesman*, 8 February 1980.
65. *Africa* no 105, May 1980.
66. Ranger, *op. cit*. p. 18.

3. The Ambiguous Victory 52-71

1. See the correspondence in the *Times* on 18 and 21 August 1980 for evidence supporting this interpretation.
2. *RH*, 25 February 1980.
3. Quoted in Catholic Institute for International Relations, 'Rhodesia: some notes on the current situation', 1 February 1980, p. 9.
4. *Zimbabwe-Rhodesia: Proposals for Independence*, Cmd.R.ZR. no. 18, 1979, Salisbury: the Government Printer, 1979, p. 25.
5. See D. Caute, 'Thugs in coffee-coloured shirts', *New Statesman* 29 February 1980, for an excellent summary of the conditions under which ZANU-PF had to work during the elections.
6. Interview with Alex Callinicos and David Caute, 26 February 1980.
7. Interview with Alex Callinicos, 26 February 1980.
8. L. Cliffe, 'The Zimbabwe elections', *RAPE* no. 15/16, p. 127.
9. Jonathan Steele in *Guardian*, 27 February 1980.

10. B.H. Masanu, 'The Zimbabwe independence elections in Mashonaland Central Province', Conference on Zimbabwe, Leeds University, 21-22 June 1980.
11. J.M.M. Mpofu, 'The February 1980 Zimbabwe elections: the Matabeleland North and South Provinces', Conference on Zimbabwe, Leeds University, 21-22 June 1980.
12. *Times*, 5 March 1980.
13. *RH*, 25 February 1980.
14. *Times*, 5 March 1980.
15. *Ibid.* 22 March 1980.
16. P.S. Harris, *Black Industrial Workers in Rhodesia*, Gwelo: Mambo Press, 1974, pp. 54-8.
17. *Herald*, 5 May 1980.
18. *Ibid.* 6 May 1980.
19. *FT*, 29 May 1980.
20. *Ibid.* 13 June 1980.
21. R. Riddell, *The Land Question in Rhodesia*, Gwelo: Mambo Press, 1980, p. 54.
22. *FT*, 'Survey on Zimbabwe', 22 April 1980.
23. See Riddell, *op. cit.* pp. 63-72.
24. See D.G. Clarke, *Agricultural and Plantation Workers in Rhodesia*, Gwelo: Mambo Press, 1977, chapters II and IX.
25. R. Riddell, 'Alternative development strategies for Zimbabwe', 'Issues in development' seminar, Centre for Interracial Studies, University of Rhodesia, 18 February 1980, p. 10.
26. See C. Leys, *Underdevelopment in Kenya*, London: Heinemann, 1975, chapter 3.
27. Interview in *FT*, 'Survey on Zimbabwe', 22 April 1980.
28. D.G. Clarke, *Foreign Companies and International Investment in Zimbabwe* (London and Gwelo: CIIR/Mambo Press, 1980) pp. 168, 32, 61.
29. *FT*, 'Survey on Zimbabwe', 22 April 1980.
30. *Herald*, 6 May 1980.
31. *FM*, 16 May 1980.
32. *Herald*, 1 May 1980
33. *Times*, 22 March 1980.
34. Quoted in *FT*, 'Survey on Zimbabwe', 22 April 1980.
35. *FT*, 17 July 1980.
36. *FM*, 18 April 1980.
37. *Guardian*, 15 August 1980.
38. *Times* , 31 July 1980.
39. *Ibid.*, 20 June 1980.
40. *Newsweek*, 6 October 1980.
41. R. Luxemburg, 'Reform or Revolution', in *Rosa Luxemburg Speaks,* New York: Pathfinder, 1970, pp. 77-8.
42. Quoted in J. Saul, 'Zimbabwe: the next round', Conference on Zimbabwe, Leeds University, 21-22 June 1980.
43. Interview with *FT*, Survey on Zimbabwe, 22 April 1980.
44. Interview with Alex Callinicos, 26 February 1980.
45. *Ibid.*
46. C. Ashton, 'The future of black business', *Commerce*, February 1980.
47. See D.G. Clarke, *Agricultural and Plantation Workers in Rhodesia*, pp. 90-5.
48. See the illuminating discussion in C. Leys, 'Capital accumulation, class formation and dependency — the significance of the Kenyan case', *The Socialist Register, 1978*, London: Merlin, 1978.
49. Harris, *op. cit.*, p. 14.
50. D.G. Clarke, *Foreign Companies and International Investment in Zimbabwe*, p. 137.

51. See T. Cliff, 'Deflected permament revolution', *IS*, no. 61.
52. Interview in *Financial Weekly*, 2 May 1980.
53. *Times*, 3 and 4 November 1980.
54. *Observer*, 13 July 1980.
55. *FM*, 4 April 1980.
56. *Ibid.* 25 April 1980.
57. *FT*, 6 August 1980.
58. *Ibid.* 17 July 1980.
59. *Economist*, 16 August 1980.
60. *Times*, 13 August 1980.

4. South Africa — the roots of the crisis 72-92

1. V.I. Lenin, *Collected Works*, vol. 13, Moscow: Progress Publishers, 1972, p. 239. See also Barrington Moore Jr., *Social Origins of Dictatorship and Dcmocracy*, Harmondsworth: Penguin, 1969. The analysis in this chapter and the following is heavily indebted to the so-called 'neo-marxist' school of South African historiography, and in particular the work of Martin Legassick and his collaborators. It would not be appropriate to discuss here the methodological issues that have divided this school between those, such as Legassick, who give primacy to the contradiction between capital and labour and the group influenced by Nicos Poulantzas who accord greater weight to conflicts between different 'fractions' of capital. On these questions see S. Clarke, 'Capital, fractions of capital and the state', *Capital and Class* no. 5, Summer 1978, and, for a discussion which does not refer specifically to South Africa but covers some of the same ground, A. Callinicos, *Is There a Future for Marxism?*, London: Macmillan, 1981. Some of the main texts dealing with the background to this section are: F.A. Johnstone, 'White prosperity and white supremacy in South Africa today', *African Affairs*, 69:275, April 1970, and *Race, Class and Gold*, London; Routledge and Kegan Paul, 1976; S. Trapido, 'South Africa in a comparative study of industrialisation', *Journal of Development Studies*, 7:3, April 1971; H. Woipe, 'Capitalism and cheap labour-power in South Africa', *Economy and Society*, 1:4, November 1972; M. Legassick, 'South Africa: capital accumulation and violence', *ibid.* 3:3, August 1974, and 'Legislation, ideology and economy in post-1948 South Africa', *JSAS*, 1:1, October 1974; M. Williams, 'An analysis of South African capitalism', *Bulletin of the Conference of Socialist Economists*, IV:1, February 1975; D. O'Meara, 'The 1946 mineworkers strike and the political economy of South Africa', *Journal of Comparative and Commonwealth Studies*, XII, 1975; M.L. Morris, 'Capitalism in South African agriculture', *Economy and Society*, 5:3, August 1976; *RAPE* No. 7, special issue on South Africa; M. Legassick and D. Innes, 'Capital restructuring and apartheid', *African Affairs*, 76:305, October 1977; D. Innes, 'The mining industry in the context of South Africa's development', *ICS*, vol. 21, 1977-8; R. Christie, ' "Slim Jannie" and the forces of production', *ibid.* vol. 22, 1978-9; D. Innes and M. Plaut, 'Class struggle and the state', *RAPE, no. 11;* C. Bundy, *The Rise and Fall of the South African Peasantry*, London: Heinemann, 1980; S. Greenburg, *Race and State in Capitalist Development*, New Haven and London: Yale University Press, 1980.
2. The most comprehensive survey of the apartheid laws is the *Report of the Commission of Inquiry into Legislation affecting the Utilisation of Manpower*, RP32/1979, Pretoria: the Government Printer, 1979 (hereinafter: the Riekert report).

3. Quoted *ibid*. p. 36.
4. Quoted in J. Kane Berman, *The Method in the Madness*, London: Pluto, 1979, p. 239.
5. G. Lanning with M. Mueller, *Africa Undermined*, Harmondsworth: Penguin, 1979, pp. 148-49.
6. D.H. Houghton, *The South African Economy*, Cape Town: Oxford University Press, 1973.
7. J. Suckling, R. Weiss, D. Innes, *The Economic Factor*, Uppsala: African Publications Trust, 1975, Table 11, p. 181.
8. Quoted in Legassick, 'Legislation, ideology and economy in post-1948 South Africa', pp. 10, 11.
9. Nedbank Group Economic Unit, *South Africa: An economic appraisal*, Johannesburg: The Nedbank Group, 1977, p. 5.
10. See, for example, F.H. Cardoso, 'Dependence and development in Latin America', *New Left Review*, no. 74 July-August 1972.
11. *FM*, 11 March 1977.
12. *South Africa: an economic appraisal*, *op. cit*. p. 16.
13. *FM*, 25 April 1980.
14. G. Airovich, 'The comparative advantage of South Africa as measured by export shares', *South African Journal of Economics*, 47:2, June 1979.
15. Johannesburg *Sunday Times*, 26 February 1979.
16. M. Bienfield and D. Innes, 'Capital accumulation and South Africa', *RAPE*, no. 7, p. 31.
17. *FM*, 23 March 1979.
18. C.J. Swanepoel and J. van Dyk, 'The fixed capital stock and sectoral capital-output ratios of South Africa', *South African Reserve Bank Quarterly Bulletin*, September 1978, p. 37.
19. *FM*, 11 February 1977.
20. *Survey of Race Relations in South Africa, 1978*, Johannesburg: South African Institute of Race Relations, 1979, p. 210.
21. N. Harris, 'The Asian boom economies and the "impossibility" of national economic development', *IS*, 2:3, Winter 1978-9, p. 2.
22. *FM*, 27 April 1979.
23. D. Innes, D. O'Meara, 'Class formation and ideology: the Transkei region', *RAPE*, no. 7.
24. *Times*, 11 August 1980.
25. M. Legassick, H. Wolpe, 'The Bantustans and capital accumulation in South Africa', *RAPE*, no. 7.
26. Kane-Berman, *op. cit*. p. 244.
27. Swanepoel and van Dyk, *op. cit*. pp. 31-2.
28. *FM*, 26 August 1977.
29. *Ibid*. 19 January 1979.
30. A.D. Wassenaar, *Assault on Private Enterprise*, Cape Town: Tafelburg, 1977, p. 86.
31. *South Africa, 1979*, Johannesburg: Van Rensburg Publications, 1980, p. 371.
32. *Report of the Commission of Inquiry into Labour Legislation: Part 1 — Key Issues*, RP47/1979, Pretoria: the Government Printer, 1979, (hereinafter: the Wiehahn report) pp. 2, 1.
33. The *locus classicus* of discussion of deskilling is H. Braverman, *Labour and Monopoly Capital*, New York and London: Monthly Review Press, 1974.
34. See H. Wolpe, 'The "white working class" in South Africa', *Economy and Society*, vol. 5, no. 2, May 1976. The expression 'new middle class' has a purely descriptive meaning here. We do not agree with those South African marxists — Wolpe, Rob Davies and others — who have argued that white wage-earners in South Africa are part of the 'new petty bourgeoisie' rather than the working class. 'The

defining structural characteristic of the proletariat in Marx's analysis of capitalism is the *socio-economic compulsion to sell one's labour-power*. (E. Mandel, 'Introduction' to K. Marx, *Capital* vol. 2, Harmondsworth: Penguin, 1978, p. 47). In this sense, the mass of white wage-earners are members of the South African proletariat, even if capital and the state have been able to divide the working-class along racial lines. See the discussion of how this came to be in Innes and Plaut, 'Class struggle and the state'.

35. Wiehahn report, *op. cit.* p. 1.
36. R. Davies, 'Capital restructuring and the modification of the racial division of labour in South Africa', *JSAS*, 5:2, April 1979, pp. 183-6.
37. D. Hemson, 'Trade unionism and the struggle for liberation in South Africa', *Capital and Class*, no. 6, Autumn 1978.
38. Institute for Industrial Education, *The Durban Strikes*, Durban-Johannesburg, 1976, pp. 144-45.
39. Wiehahn report, p. 15.
40. J. Natrass, 'The narrowing of wage differentials in South Africa', *South African Journal of Economics*, 45:4, December 1977.
41. Hemson, *op. cit.* p. 30.
42. *FM*, 11 February 1977.
43. *Ibid.* 1 October 1976.
44. See Counter-Information Services, *Black South Africa Explodes*, London, 1977; *A Survey of Race Relations in South Africa, 1976*, Johannesburg: South African Institute of Race Relations, 1977; D. Herbstein, *White Man We Want to Talk to You*, Harmondsworth: Penguin, 1977; Kane-Berman, *op. cit.*; B. Hirson, *Year of Fire, Year of Ash*, London: Zed Press, 1979; A. Brooks and J. Brickhill, *Whirlwind Before the Storm*, London: International Defence and Aid Fund, 1980.
45. A. Callinicos and J. Rogers, *Southern Africa after Soweto,* London: Pluto, 1977, p. 164.
46. Hemson, *op. cit.* p. 31.
47. Kane-Berman, *op. cit.* p. 52.
48. *FM*, 6 May 1977.
49. See Callinicos and Rogers, *op. cit.* pp. 168-73, and Hirson, *op. cit.*

5. Rationalising apartheid — Piet Botha's 'Total Strategy' 93-115

1. A. Gramsci, *Selections from the Prison Notebooks*, London: Lawrence and Wishart, 1971, p. 178.
2. D. Kaplan, 'Relations of production, class struggle and the state in South Africa in the inter-war period', *RAPE*, 15/16, p. 142.
3. See R. Davies, *Capital, State and White Labour in South Africa 1900-1960*, Hassocks: the Harvester Press, 1979.
4. The best study of contemporary Afrikanerdom is H. Adam and H. Gilliomee, *Ethnic Power Mobilised*, New Haven and London: Yale University Press, 1979.
5. *Ibid.* pp. 163-73.
6. *FT*, 29 February 1980.
7. A. Callinicos and J. Rogers, *Southern Africa after Soweto*, London: Pluto, 1977 pp. 165-66.
8. See D. O'Meara, 'The Afrikaner Broederbond', *JSAS*, 3:2; and 'Analysing Afrikaner nationalism', *African Affairs*, 77:306, January 1978.
9. J.H.P. Serfontein, *Brotherhood of Power*, London: Rex Collings, 1979, p. 107.
10. *Ibid.* pp. 176-77.
11. E. Potter, *The Press as Opposition*, London: Chatto and Windus, 1975, pp. 151, 183, 189-90, 199.

12. Adam and Gilliomee, *op. cit.* p. 87.
13. See *Report of the Commission of Inquiry into Alleged Irregularities in the Former Department of Information*, RP113/1978, Pretoria: the Government Printer, 1978, and the commission's *Supplementary Report* RP63/1979, Pretoria: the Government Printer, 1979.
14. A. Wassenaar, *Assault on Private Enterprise*, Cape Town: Tafelburg, 1979, p. 119.
15. *FM*, 25 June 1979.
16. *The Apartheid War Machine*, London: International Defence and Aid Fund, 1980.
17. G-A Fiechter, *Brazil since 1964*, London: Macmillan, 1975, p. 29.
18. J.A. Lombard, 'The economic aspects of national security', in M.H.H. Louw (ed.), *National Security: A Modern Approach*, Pretoria: Institute of Strategic Studies, 1978, p. 85.
19. *Economist*, 21 October 1978.
20. See *Newsweek*, 29 September 1980.
21. J.R. Dutton, 'The military aspects of national security', in Louw (ed.), *op. cit.* pp. 107, 114.
22. *The Apartheid War Machine*, pp. 6-7.
23. Wassenaar, *op. cit.* pp. 148-50.
24. *South African Reserve Bank Quarterly Bulletin*, March 1980.
25. *FM*, 4 April 1980. The *Financial Mail*, hitherto one of the regime's most intelligent capitalist critics, underwent a sad degeneration after the installation in 1979 of a new editor, a committed monetarist and author of a book called *Milton Friedman in South Africa*!
26. *Ibid.* 3 August 1979.
27. Lombard, p. 86.
28. *Report of the Commission of Inquiry into Legislation affecting the Utilisation of Manpower*, RP32/1979, Pretoria: the Government Printer 1979, (hereinafter the Riekert Report) p. 167.
29. *FM*, 22 June 1980.
30. J. Kane-Berman, *South Africa — the Method in the Madness*, London: Pluto 1979, p. 234.
31. Riekert Report, p. 168.
32. *Report of the Commission of Inquiry into Labour Legislation: Part I — Key Issues* RP47/1979 Pretoria: the Government Printer 1979, (hereinafter the Wiehahn Report) p. 18.
33. See R. Davies, D. Lewis, 'Industrial relations legislation: one of capital's defences', *RAPE* no. 7.
34. Wiehahn Report, pp. 18, 19.
35. *FM*, 11 May 1979.
36. H. Cheadle, 'A guide to the Industrial Conciliation Act No. 94 of 1979', *SALB*, 5:2, August 1979.
37. *FM*, 11 May 1979.
38. *Ibid.*, 18 May 1979.
39. *Ibid.*, 25 January 1980.
40. *Ibid.*, 15 June 1979.
41. Interview in A. Starke, *Survival*, Cape Town: Tafelburg 1978, pp. 155-6.
42. See R. Davies, 'Capital restructuring and the modification of the racial division of labour', *JSAS*, 5:2, April 1979.
43. See A. Sitas, 'Rebels without a pause: the MWU and the defence of the colour bar', *SALB*, 5:3, October 1979.
44. See C. Cooper, 'The mineworkers' strike', *ibid.*
45. Interview in Starke, *op. cit.* p. 128.
46. *FM*, 3 December 1976.
47. *Ibid.* 15 June 1979.
48. *Ibid.* 13 July 1979.
49. *Ibid.* 14 September 1979.

50. *Ibid.* 13 June 1980.
51. *Ibid.* 21 September 1979.
52. *Ibid.* 14 September 1979.
53. *Ibid.* 20 July 1979.
54. Lombard, *op. cit.* pp. 92, 93.
55. Interview in Starke, *op. cit.* pp. 155-6.
56. *Ibid.* p. 177.
57. *FM*, 30 November 1979.
58. Adam and Gilliomee, *op. cit.* p. 204.
59. Cf. survey in the *Times*, 4 July 1980.
60. *FM*, 22 June 1979.
61. *Times*, 2 and 3 September 1980.
62. Adam and Gilliomee, *op. cit.* pp. 221-32.
63. *Ibid.* pp. 165-6.
64. *FM*, 9 November 1979.
65. See F. Parkin, *Marxism and Class Theory*, London: Tavistock 1979.
66. *FM*, 16 November 1979.
67. Quoted in *The Apartheid War Machine*, *op. cit.* p. 7.
68. Wassenaar, *op. cit.* p. 153.
69. Dutton, *op. cit.* p. 113.
70. See N. Poulantzas, *Fascisme et Dictature*, Paris: Seuil 1970.

6. The Third Round — Workers and Students Challenge Botha 116-141

1. A. Wassenaar, *Assault on Private Enterprise* Cape Town: Tafelburg 1977, p. 14.
2. *South African Reserve Bank Quarterly Bulletin*, March 1980.
3. G. de Kock, 'The business cycle in South Africa — recent tendencies', *South African Journal of Economics*, 43:1, March 1975.
4. See A. Callinicos and J. Rogers, *Southern Africa after Soweto*, London: Pluto 1977; and R.W. Johnson, *How Long will South Africa Survive?* London: Macmillan 1977.
5. 'Shifting Sands', International Banking: a survey, *Economist* 22 March 1980.
6. *Ibid.*
7. See, for example, *FT*, 4 January 1980. Some monetarists — for example, the editor of *The Times*, William Rees-Mogg — advocate a return to the gold standard.
8. E. Mandel, *The Second Slump*, London: NLB/Verso 1980, p. 218.
9. *FM*, 'Special Survey on Gold', 30 May 1980.
10. *FT*, 25 June 1980.
11. *FM*, 11 May 1980.
12. *FT*, 29 August 1980.
13. *FM*, 22 February 1980.
14. *Ibid.* 15 June 1979, 21 January 1977.
15. *Economist*, 8 March 1980.
16. *FM*, 4 April 1980.
17. *Ibid.* 30 May 1980 and 6 April 1979.
18. 'The Great Evasion', South Africa: a survey, *Economist*, 21 June 1980.
19. *FM*, 17 August 1979.
20. *Ibid.* 28 September 1979.
21. *Ibid.* 9 November 1979.
22. *Ibid.* 11 January 1980.
23. *Work in Progress*, 11, February 1980.
24. *FM*, 2 March 1979.
25. *Ibid.* 2 November 1979.
26. 'The Great Evasion' *op. cit.* p. 19.

27. *FM*, 14 December 1979.
28. *Ibid.* 18 January 1979.
29. *Ibid.* 13 July 1979.
30. *Ibid.* 30 November 1979.
31. *Report of the Commission of Inquiry into Labour Legislation Part 1 — Key Issues*, RP47/1979, Pretoria: Government Printer 1979, (hereinafter the Wiehahn report) pp. 30-33.
32. *FM*, 4 November 1977.
33. P. Hendler, 'The organisation of parallel unions', *SALB*, 5:6 & 7, March 1980, p. 107.
34. See FOSATU, 'Memorandum on the Parallel Union Thrust', *ibid.*
35. Wiehahn report, p. 22.
36. *FM*, 18 May 1979.
37. *Ibid.* 28 September 1979.
38. WPGWU, 'Memorandum', *SALB*, 5:4.
39. *FM*, 12 October 1979.
40. FOSATU, 'Statement', *SALB*, 5: 6 & 7, March 1980.
41. This account draws on the *SALB* 6:2 and 3, special issue on Ford, September 1980 and an interview with Thozamile Botha, 5 November 1980.
42. *FM*, 23 November 1979.
43. See S. Greenburg, *Race and State in Capitalist Development*, New Haven and London: Yale University Press 1980, chapter 14.
44. *Work in Progress* 11, February 1980, p. 15.
45. *FM*, 30 November 1979.
46. *Work in Progress, op. cit.* p. 18.
47. *FM*, 21 December 1979.
48. M. Nicol, 'Legislation, registration, emasculation', *SALB*, 5: 6 & 7, March 1980, pp. 52, 51.
49. I. Wilkins and J. Strydom, *The Broederbond*, New York and London: Paddington Press 1979 pp. 170-74.
50. *FM*, 23 April 1980.
51. *Ibid.* 28 September 1979.
52. *Ibid.* 9 May 1980.
53. See University of Stellenbosch survey, reported *ibid.* 5 October 1979.
54. *FT*, 19 June 1980.
55. *FM*, 9 May 1980.
56. *Ibid.* 16 November 1979. See also L. McGregor, 'The Fatti's and Moni's strike', *SALB*, 5: 6 & 7, March 1980.
57. WPGWU, 'Registration, recognition and organisation: the case of the Cape Town stevedores', *ibid.*
58. *FM*, 25 April 1980.
59. *Survey of Race Relations in South Africa, 1978*, Johannesburg: South African Institute of Race Relations 1979, p. 399.
60. This account follows that in 'The school boycott', *Social Review*, no. 9, May 1980.
61. *Times*, 18 April 1980.
62. *FT*, 19 June 1980.
63. *Times*, 4 July 1980.
64. A. Hirsch, 'An introduction to textile workers' organisation in Natal', *SALB*, 4:8, January/February 1979.
65. See *FM*, 30 May 1980; and *Times*, 4 July 1980.
66. *FT*, 14 July 1980.
67. *Ibid.* 27 June 1980.
68. *Times*, 10 June 1980.
69. *Guardian*, 29 May 1980.
70. *FT*, 11 August 1980.
71. *Ibid.*
72. *Ibid.* 9 April 1980.

7. Strategy and Tactics 142-167

1. V.I. Lenin, *Collected Works*, vol. 31, Moscow: Progress Publishers 1966, pp. 84-85.
2. *Star*, 14 August 1976.
3. See D. Innes, D. O'Meara, 'Class formation and ideology: the Transkei region', *RAPE*, no. 7.
4. *FM*, 18 May 1979.
5. By 'Toussaint', a SACP theoretician, in a rather abusive and libellous review of *Southern Africa after Soweto*, 'Class and nation in the South African revolution', *AC* no. 72, First Quarter 1978.
6. See 'Prepare the theoretical foundations for the building of the vanguard party', *The way forward*, no. 2, First Quarter 1978.
7. Editorial, *The way forward*, no. 3, Second Quarter 1978.
8. S. Biko, *I write what I like*, London: Heinemann 1979, p. 29.
9. V.I. Lenin, *Collected Works*, vol. 22, Moscow: Progress Publishers, 1964, pp. 355-56.
10. G. Gerhart, *Black Power in South Africa*, Berkeley and London: University of California Press 1978, pp. 317-20.
11. These are points stressed by Baruch Hirson in *Year of Fire, Year of Ash*, London: Zed Press 1979.
12. Quoted in Gerhart, *op. cit.* p. 60.
13. Biko, *op. cit.* pp. 20-21, 83.
14. *Ibid.* pp. 89, 97, 134, 136.
15. A. Brooks and J. Brickhill, *Whirlwind before the Storm*, London: International Defence and Aid Fund 1980, p. 89.
16. Hirson's hostility to the black consciousness movement leads him to exaggerate greatly the role of the ANC in the Soweto uprising. Even the reviewer of Hirson's book in the SACP journal felt obliged to protest that his attitude to the BCM was 'an indication that he had not appreciated it as the first and necessary stage towards a higher political and ideological understanding of the complexities of the South African revolution', *AC*, no. 81, Second Quarter 1980.
17. *A Survey of Race Relations in South Africa, 1978*, Johannesburg: South African Institute of Race Relations 1979 (hereinafter *Survey*) pp. 32-33.
18. *FM*, 22 July 1977.
19. A. Starke, *Survival*, Cape Town: Tafelburg 1978, pp. 117-18.
20. 'The Great Evasion', South Africa: a survey, *Economist*, 21 June 1980.
21. *Survey*, *op. cit.* p. 36.
22. N.S. Nyameko and G. Singh, 'The role of black consciousness in the South African revolution', *AC* no. 68, First Quarter 1977, p. 46.
23. 'The way forward from Soweto', *AC* no. 70, Third Quarter 1977, pp. 41, 42.
24. See *The workers movement, SACTU and ANC*, London, 1980.
25. See W. Jones, 'Problems of the Ethiopian revolution', *AC* no. 69, Fourth Quarter 1977 (compare 'A historic advance — the founding of the Somali Revolutionary Socialist Party', *AC* no. 68, First Quarter 1977) and 'Statement of the central committee of the South African Communist Party on the situation in Afghanistan, *AC* no. 81, Second Quarter 1980.
26. *FM*, 9 November 1979.
27. E. Webster, 'A profile of unregistered union members in Natal', *SALB*, 4:8, January-February 1979.
28. *FM*, 6 July 1979.
29. London *Sunday Times*, 4 May 1980.
30. Interview in Starke, *op. cit.* p. 79.
31. Hirson, *op. cit.* p. 244.

32. Brooks and Brickhill, *op. cit.* pp. 215-24, 226.
33. *Survey*, *op. cit.* p. 31.
34. *FM*, 9 November 1979.
35. *FT*, 14 March 1980.
36. J. Kane-Berman, *The Method in the Madness*, London: Pluto 1979, p. 212.
37. *Times*, 19 August 1980.
38. *Ibid.*
39. *FT*, 3 June 1980.
40. Anti-Apartheid Movement, *The Battle for South Africa*, National Action Conference on Southern Africa after Zimbabwe, 31 May 1980, p. 1.
41. Kane-Berman, *op. cit.* p. 219.
42. *The Battle for South Africa*, *op. cit.* pp. 14-15.
43. Quoted, *ibid.* p. 4.
44. *FM*, 26 October 1979.
45. *Survey*, p. 303.
46. *FM*, 7 September 1979.
47. Innes and O'Meara, *op. cit.*
48. *FM*, 18 May 1979.
49. 'The Great Evasion', *op. cit.* p. 25.
50. *Ibid.* p. 24.
51. R. Thompson, *Defeating Communist Insurgency*, London: Chatto and Windus 1965, p. 51.
52. *FM*, 17 August 1979.
53. *Ibid.* 11 May 1979.
54. *Ibid.* 30 November 1979.
55. *Times*, 9 August 1980.
56. 'Comrade Mzala', 'Armed struggle in South Africa', *AC* no. 82, Third Quarter 1980, pp 67, 68, 70.
57. *The workers movement, SACTU and ANC*, p. 43.
58. K. Marx and F. Engels, *Selected Correspondence*, Moscow: Progress Publishers 1955, p. 92.
59. *The workers movement, SACTU and ANC*, *op. cit.* p. 35. There is a perceptive critique of this pamphlet, 'The role of trade unions in the South African revolution', by 'A reader' in the SACP journal, *AC*, no. 82, Third Quarter 1980.
60. Quoted in J. Maree, 'The Port Elizabeth strikes and an evaluation of the UAW', *SALB*, 6: 2 and 3, September 1980 p. 27.
61. Interview with Alex Callinicos, 5 November 1980.
62. V.I. Lenin, *What is to be Done?*, *Collected Works*, vol. 5, Moscow: Progress Publishers 1961, p. 423.

Abbreviations

AC	*African Communist* (London)
FM	*Financial Mail* (Johannesburg)
FT	*Financial Times* (London)
ICS	University of London Institute of Commonwealth Studies Collected Seminar Papers
IS	*International Socialism* (London)
JSAS	*Journal of Southern African Studies* (Oxford)
RAPE	*Review of African Political Economy* (London)
RH	*Rhodesia Herald* (Salisbury), renamed *The Herald* in August 1978.
SALB	*Southern African Labour Bulletin* (Durban)

Index